A PRAYER
FOR THE PRAIRIE

Learning Faith on a Small Farm

Raylene Frankhauser Nickel

Foreword by John Ikerd

Five Penny Press
Kief, North Dakota

Five Penny Press
3117 5th Ave. NE
Kief, North Dakota 58723-9500
www.fivepennypress.com

Excerpts from *The Unsettling of America: Culture & Agriculture* by Wendell Berry. Copyright ©1997 by Wendell Berry. Reprinted by permission of Sierra Club Books and Wendell Berry.

Excerpts from *Crazy Musings from the North Outback* by Terry Jacobson. Reprinted by permission of the author.

Excerpts from "Feeding the Village First" by Fred Kirschenmann. Reprinted by permission of the Northern Plains Sustainable Agriculture Society.

Excerpts from *Holistic Management: a New Framework for Decision Making* by Allan Savory and Jody Butterfield. Copyright ©1999 by Allan Savory. Reprinted by permission of Island Press and the Allan Savory Center for Holistic Management.

Excerpts from *Wild Hope* by Tom Sine. Copyright ©1991 by Tom Sine. Reprinted by permission of the author.

Scripture quotations are from the Revised Standard Version of the Bible, copyright ©1946, 1952, and 1971 by the Division of Christian Education of the National Council of the Churches of Christ in the USA. Used by permission. All rights reserved.

Publisher's Cataloging-in-Publication
(Provided by Quality Books, Inc.)

Frankhauser Nickel, Raylene.
    A prayer for the prairie: learning faith on a small farm / Raylene Frankhauser Nickel; foreword by John Ikerd.
    p. cm.
    Includes bibliographical references and index.
    LCCN 2003112780
    ISBN 0-9746108-0-1

    1. Frankhauser Nickel, Raylene. 2. Nickel, John. 3. Farm life–Great Plains–Biography. 4. Farm life–Great Plains–Religious aspects–Christianity. 5. Farm life–Great Plains–History. 6. Agriculture–Economic aspects–Great Plains–History. 7. Great Plains–Social conditions. I. Title.

    S417.F7146A3 2004   630'.978
                        QBI33-1647

Printed in the United States of America
(See *RESOURCES FOR READERS* for printer name and address.)

For my husband, John, who has coauthored this book through our long talks, his imagination, and the everyday work of his hands. Thank you for your belief.

This book, too, is for the memory of my father and mother, Roy and Algona Frankhauser, who lived out their lives on the prairie. I will always be thankful that my father was a man of prayer, and that he set me behind the collar of one of his Belgian workhorses when I was a child. I will always be thankful, too, that my mother believed in farming, and that she encouraged me to write.

To my sister, Karen, and my brother, John: Thank you for prayers and words that heal.

ACKNOWLEDGMENTS

I owe much to the more than one thousand farmers, ranchers, and other agricultural professionals who have shared their thoughts and experiences with me during my 20 years of writing for regional and national agricultural publications. Since all have contributed to my cumulative experience, each has had a hand in the shaping of this book.

To Allan Savory's books and insights John and I owe a great debt. For from him we learned to look beneath the surface.

From the writings of Wendell Berry we learned to value the work of our hands and to see the many layers of potential prosperity inherent in the running of a home and a farm.

Many people encouraged the writing of this work, and I am deeply indebted to them all. A number of readers helped shape the final outcome of the book through their insightful guidance. Thank you.

Todd Spichke, a son of the Dakota prairie, created the cover design when this physical book was but a vision. His artful work surely served as a beacon, drawing the book finally to fruition.

Thanks to C.J. Hadley of *Range* magazine for publishing excerpts of *A Prayer for the Prairie* while it was a work in progress.

CONTENTS

FOREWORD

by John Ikerd

American agriculture is in a time of great transition. Transitions are times of change; and change, more often than not, is painful. While the old era of agriculture is suffering the pains of death, a new era is struggling through the pains of birth. However, without the pains of death and birth, the hope and joy of new life would be but a dream. Nothing lives forever. The only concept of sustainability we know is that of renewal, reproduction, and regeneration—of continuing cycles of death and rebirth.

This book is a story of two people who have grieved the loss of old ways of thinking and of farming but have found hope in new ways of thinking that promise new and better ways of farming for the future. This book, perhaps better than any I have read, addresses the issue of building a sustainable philosophy of life, which is the most critical issue in building a sustainable agriculture and a sustainable society.

Anyone who has lived on a farm anywhere during the past 50 years will find much familiar in *A Prayer for the Prairie*. The joys and hardships of a life lived among the things of nature on a family farm is a classic American theme. Raylene Frankhauser Nickel articulates this theme more picturesquely, yet more clearly, than do most writers—perhaps because each word actually comes from her heart. This book will be thoroughly enjoyed by many because it stirs memories and emotions most of us keep buried yet long for someone to pull back to the surface of our minds.

But this is not a book of nostalgia for farm and ranch life of the past. Rather, it is a book of new hope for the future of farmers and ranchers everywhere. This book is about nurturing a new, sustainable way of farming, which promises a better quality of life on the land for all who are willing to learn to live and work in harmony with nature.

The story of difficulties, frustrations, and failures of Raylene and John Nickel is a classic story of the twentieth-century family farm. Financial crisis has been a chronic characteristic of American agriculture. Periods of relative prosperity have been few and short-lived. American farmers have been the victims of their own productivity, which has produced chronic overproduction. An endless succession of new technologies, beginning around the turn of the last century with mechanization, made it possible for fewer farmers to produce more, decade after decade. Tractors removed the power constraints of horse farming, and commercial fertilizers and pesticides removed the management constraints of diversified farming. Today, farmers are told that new biological and informational technologies will remove all constraints of nature. Each of these new technologies has seemed to promise a better life for farmers, but the promises all have been empty.

Technologies gave farmers the means to specialize and standardize their operations—to make their farms work like factories. Specialization and standardization allowed farmers to mechanize and routinize their operations, making it possible for each farmer to farm more land, raise more livestock—to operate a bigger farm. In fact, farmers had to become larger, at first to recoup their investments in new technologies, and then, just to survive. Each new production method promised to reduce farmers' per-unit cost of production, and thus, to increase profit margins—but only if each farmer produced more.

However, only the early innovators realized any real benefits, and even then, often not enough to pay for their new investments. As more and more individual farmers adopted a new machine, new chemical, new breed of animal, or new variety of crop, total production of the affected commodity increased, and invariably, prices fell. Now other farmers were forced to adopt the technologies—not for profits but for survival.

Those farmers who didn't adopt soon enough, often because of circumstances beyond their control, didn't survive. Their land and their place in agriculture had to be given up so the fewer surviving farmers could consolidate more land and capital under their control. As a result, farmers achieved the "economies of scale" that arise from the process of industrialization.

The experts have found ways to blame the farmers who have failed for their own demise. They were marginal producers, they borrowed too much money, or they were technological laggards, we were told. But in fact, with each new round of industrial technology, prices had to stay low enough long enough to force enough farmers out of business so the survivors could be "more efficient." Government policies, including the publicly funded research and education that developed and promoted much of the technology, were designed to increase the efficiency of agriculture—not to save the family or revitalize rural communities. Thus, the struggles and difficulties of the Nickels epitomize the life of the typical American farm family caught up in an agricultural transition over which they had no control.

Technology per se was not the problem. It's simply that the industrial technologies of the past made farmers less necessary rather than actually enhancing their productivity. There was a time when the industrialization of agriculture made sense. America needed people to work in the factories and offices of a growing industrial economy, and Americans needed to reduce the claim of food and fiber on their disposable incomes. We simply didn't anticipate the negative ecological and social consequences of an industrial agriculture. Today, however, we are shipping our good-paying factory jobs to other countries, where people will work harder for less money, leaving America with a chronic surplus of workers.

The average American today spends a little more than a dime of each dollar of disposable income for food, and the farmer gets less than a penny of that dime. The rest goes to marketing and input supply firms. Today, society has little to gain, and much to lose, from the continued industrialization of agriculture.

A PRAYER FOR THE PRAIRIE

Raylene Frankhauser Nickel tells this story of American agriculture from the perspective of a farmer who has lived it. This is a story from which all farmers and ranchers can benefit. Farmers need to understand that the problems they have experienced, at least in most cases, have not been their fault. They also need to understand that their situation will not be made better by another round of industrial technologies. But more importantly, farmers who are caught on the technology treadmill today need to join the Nickels and other farmers like them who have stepped off the treadmill and are breaking a new trail toward a new and better kind of agriculture for the future.

This is a story, too, from which we all, as consumers and citizens, can benefit. Today, the dwindling potential economic benefits from further industrialization are far less than the growing ecological and social risks. Resources critical to the future of human life on earth—soil, water, air—are being depleted and degraded by mono-cropping, unwise pesticide and fertilizer use, confinement animal feeding, excessive irrigation, and now, genetic engineering. Growing concerns for food safety and nutrition are direct consequences of an industrial food system. And today, giant multinational corporations are gaining control of the global food supply "from dirt to the dinner plate," mostly through comprehensive production contracts.

The current industrial systems of farming and food production quite simply are not sustainable. All people, as producers, consumers and citizens, have a critical responsibility to encourage, support, even demand, more sustainable systems of farming and food production.

I like to think of sustainable farming as common sense farming. A sustainable farm is a farm that can last. If a farm degrades its resources base—soil, air, or water—the farm eventually will lose its ability to produce, and thus, is not sustainable. If a farm goes broke, the farmer loses his or her right to make decisions about how the land is used, and thus, the farm is not sustainable. And, if a farm doesn't meet the needs of society, it will not be supported by society, and thus, the farm is not sustainable. A sustainable agriculture must meet the needs of the present while leaving equal or better opportunities for the future. Thus, a sustainable farm must be ecologically sound, economically viable, and socially responsible—it's just common sense.

Wendell Berry, Allan Savory, and Fred Kirschenmann—all quoted extensively in this book—are among the visionaries of this new, sustainable way of farming. But farmers, like Raylene and John Nickel, are the actual creators of this new agriculture. Hundreds of thousands of these new farmers, all across the continent and around the world, are breathing new life into agriculture. They are pioneers on the frontier of farming, and life is rarely easy on the frontiers of change. They continue to confront frustrations and risk of failure. But more and more are finding ways to succeed.

These new farmers are learning to farm in harmony with nature, rather than trying to conquer nature. They are harvesting solar energy and reducing their reliance on nonrenewable fossil energy. They are caring for the land so it will care for them. They help each other succeed, rather than drive each other out of business. They produce for customers who want foods produced differently from the industrial foods they find in supermarkets or fast-food restaurants, and they receive premium prices for their efforts. They are caring for others so others will care for them. But perhaps more importantly, these new farmers realize that sustainable farming must be a "way of life" as well as a way to make a living. No one expresses this kind of love of land and people more clearly than does Raylene Frankhauser Nickel in *A Prayer for the Prairie*.

Sustainable farming also requires an acceptance of a "higher order of things" to which our thoughts and actions must conform. A true commitment to sustainability must stem from the acceptance of our ethical and moral responsibility to do for those of future generations, as we would have them do for us—if we were of their generation and they were of ours. The true benefit of living sustainably is the quality of life that arises from not only caring for ourselves, but also, from our conscious, purposeful commitment to care for others and to care for the earth.

As Raylene puts it, "I do not mind that my body shows that my life is not physically easy; I do not mind that my possessions reveal that my life is not always comfortable and convenient. It is an inner smoothness that I am after, a sure sense that I am doing the work for which God has marked me . . . and that I am in my proper place. ...Where there is a calling, there is meaning. And where life has meaning, there is a deep, abiding resiliency to difficulty and uncertainty, even a good measure of peace of mind. Because of that, I feel rich."

No visionary has stated more clearly the true meaning of a sustainable quality of life than has this farmer in this book.

John Ikerd
Professor Emeritus
Agricultural Economics
University of Missouri
July 23, 2003

PREFACE

I have worked on this farm during its high days of a noontide time of financial prosperity, when my body was lithe and my spirit as high as that of the Arabian stallion with whom I raced, windblown, across the fields.

But a time of taming came, and I worked on this farm during its days of silence and slow motion, when its rivers of prosperity dried to a trickle, when its life hung in the balance, tipping more toward death than life. It was a time when I walked on foot.

Now the balance has tipped back again toward life, still precarious, yet nevertheless stirring beneath the surface in new ways, offering the hope of a new kind of life for a new time . . . and a renewed kind of place. My turbulent spirit has grown some peace because, like the prairie rose, I am learning to live on arid, unpredictable ground under the arching freedom of God's wide-open skies.

When I wrote the first chapter of this book in the winter of 1999-2000, I had no idea then—only a vision and the prayers of my Christian faith—that the final chapter, written in March 2002, would hold as much hope as it does. Buffeted as agriculture is by outer and inner forces, finding enduring, prosperous ways to live and work on a small farm on the Northern Plains has become an enigma. Indeed, at times it seems impossible. But with increasing frequency my husband, John, and I catch glimpses of the possibility of an enduring future springing from our work. More importantly, our efforts have taught us much about our relationship with God and with the land upon which we live.

In retrospect I see that these spiritual essays about life on a small farm in North Dakota comprise a work of contradictions. At first, this troubled me, and I thought that I had to resolve these incongruities so that the themes of the chapters would be woven with continuity. Yet, in the end, it seems impossible to resolve them, since human nature is, itself, full of contradictions. Truth has many faces. Throughout this work, then, these contradictions stand: We farmers stay, and yet we leave; we believe, yet we doubt; we love, and yet we act without love; we are faithful and yet faithless; we seek justice, and yet often—through the unthinking ways by which we treat the earth, our local business owners, our neighbors and indeed our own families—we oppress.

It is not my intent to thrust my Christian belief on the reader. Yet because my belief is enmeshed in the fabric of my thoughts, my experiences are filtered through it. It would not be truthful to describe my experiences without the backdrop of my Christian perspective. However, it is indeed my intent to draw the reader toward a spiritual view, particularly of rural and agricultural life. For, religious belief aside, it seems rational to assume that spiritual principles undergird all of life and that living in balance with these is key to fruitful living. Ferreting out and exploring, sometimes metaphorically, those spiritual principles that may lie at the core of the difficulties agriculture often presents farmers and ranchers and our rural communities is the point of this book. Addressing these through the individual choices comprising our daily lives is a matter of personal discovery of unique processes. Living out these discoveries is a matter of faith.

GETTING AROUND FEAR

Troubles
arising over years
nag at me
dragging me down
physically and spiritually.
Excessive rain
over nearly a decade,
damages the crops
with weeds and disease.
Fear builds in me
as finances tighten.
Though I try
to act in faith,
I move away
from this fear.
It gets bigger
and bigger.
I lose confidence,
move faster
around and around.
I want to believe,
but fear keeps haunting me,
troubles keep mounting.
It isn't fun
to farm anymore,
this profession I wanted
for my whole life.
My mind swirls faster

as my two big tractors
go down
with serious problems.
It gets so stressful.
I feel it in my health;
it nags my mind.
I can not outrun it.
I slow, as the reality
sets in,
that I must act
in faith,
stop running
and face that fear.
I must stop
talking sustainability
and move to
live it.
I stop,
I face my fear,
that I could lose
the farm.
Suddenly, opportunities
like blessings
fall in my lap,
unexpected grace.
I feel as if I've been
in a round pen
with God.

— by Terry Jacobson, Wales, North Dakota
Author of *Crazy Musings From the North Outback*
and *Big Thoughts From a Small Farmer*
(Used by permission)

A PRAYER
FOR THE PRAIRIE
1999–2000

I stand on a prairie hill. This is my favorite place of prayer. It is an early evening in midsummer, and bees drone amid the sweet clover plants growing helter-skelter on the hill. My father, my brothers, and the farmer-renters who once grew grain on the fields spilling down from this hill, all cultivated across the crown of this, the farm's highest promontory. But my husband, John, who now follows these men in the tending of the farm, refuses to till the top of the Big Hill, where the light and fragile soil is easily blown away by the wind. A nearby fence is half buried by an old grass-covered bank of drift soil, deposited there by the wind during the years when the hill was cultivated. The drift soil testifies to the hill's unwillingness to be tilled.

Since John has left the top of the hill alone, it is slowly healing itself, choosing of its own volition what vestiges of greenery to use as a cloak. The plants the hilltop voluntarily pushes forth from its yellow, clay soil are strong and hardy. They rise stalwartly from the ground each spring regardless of how fiercely winter has choked the land. They bend with the wind, shrink in the droughts, then stand up straight and green after the rains come. Amid the four-foot-high sweet clover grows a variegated understory of thin-stemmed quackgrass, gumweed, dandelions, sow thistle, and prairie roses.

The sweet clover plants are loaded with yellow blossoms breathing their fragrant scent into the eddies of the breeze as it puffs in spells across the crown of the hill, brushing my face with what seems an imperceptible yet unmistakeable caress from God. In North Dakota the air is seldom still. Indeed, wind—or lack of it—is an invisible barometer of life here, a mysterious force interwining human emotion with the power and will of the elements.

By their varying degree, time and direction, the winds soothe, energize, or inspire. In March the warm chinook winds blow steady and strong from the south, promising warm temperatures to thaw the snow. They carry hope and anticipation, a yearning for green plants growing and for the warm, pungent scent of newborn calves. In summer, the roiling wind preceding a dark thunderhead building in the western sky is invigorating. I have childhood memories of racing headlong into such a wind, with arms spread-eagled. The warm gusts filled me with such bounding energy and zeal I felt I would surely burst if I stood still. By contrast, the ripping 40-mph blizzard winds blowing from the northwest in winter bring disquietness, a sense of helplessness in the face of the wind's fury.

Indeed, I've learned from blizzards a lesson transferring to larger life. They teach the patience to wait out a battering storm. They shape the fortitude needed to peer intently at a figurative white wall of blinding, swirling snow, waiting and searching for lulls in the wind to show glimpses of my life-journey's landmarks—those signposts pointing the way in which I should walk.

Now, standing atop the Big Hill, I set my face to the eddying breeze and lose my thoughts in its gentle caress. The nearly imperceptible wind fuses the present to the past, stirring my memories. A quarter mile to the west of where I stand lies the farmstead where I was raised and where my husband, John, and I now live and work. Shelterbelts of caragana bushes and ash, elm, and cottonwood trees grow on the north and west sides of the farmstead. A single row of soaring old cottonwoods guards the east boundary of the yard. As these landmark trees have aged, some of their limbs have died, and their foliage has thinned so that, from the hill, they afford a view of the grand old farmhouse looming up from the center of the yard. The view of the house has changed little since the days of my childhood, though I am merely a few years from turning fifty. The long row of old, narrow windows peers down from the east room upstairs, and the open porch on the first floor welcomes the morning sun.

Several hundred yards northeast of the farmstead is a grove of cottonwoods that have died. The dead trees preside over a low-lying meadow. The wet weather of recent years filled the meadow with standing water, and the water soon killed the cottonwoods. Many years ago, when the trees were strong and green, and their youthful, waxy leaves made rustling sounds in the breeze like a babbling brook, I stood in their shade, reaching up to touch the velvet nostril of a horse.

I was five years old, and Mom had let me tag along to take lunch to my father, who was raking hay in the meadow with his team of big, blonde Belgian horses. While my father ate his sandwiches, the team rested in the shade of the cottonwoods. Dad handed me a bit of bread to give to one of the horses, and I put it in my flattened palm, reaching it up to the horse's big, soft nose. The horse lowered its head and gently picked the bread from my palm with its lips—but then promptly flicked the bread from its mouth. I did not care, though, that my gift had been refused, for the great horse continued to hold its head low, and I was able to stroke the velvety skin on the side of its nose.

Attached to the noseband of each horse's bridle was a broad piece of denim my mother had cut into strips. The strips hung down across the horses' nostrils and helped to keep the flies from biting the soft skin of their noses while they pulled the dump rake up and down the meadow. The rake gathered the cut-and-dried meadow grass into bunches. Later, my father would use a bucker attached to the front of a tractor to sweep up and pile these bunches into stacks of hay to feed to the livestock in winter.

A year and a half later, one evening in March, my father died in that very meadow. He had driven his team there; the horses pulled a load of manure Dad had pitched from the barn onto a stoneboat, a low, four-foot-by-eight-foot flatbed on skids. Dad's habit was to unload the manure at a stockpile in the middle of the meadow. When my father didn't come in for supper, Mom sent my older sister and brother, Karen and John, outside to search for him. They found him lying in the snow-covered meadow, the color of life drained from his gentle face.

Of course, the death of our father transformed our lives. It left a ragged hole in each of our hearts that still remains. Yet it also led to lessons teaching us how to confront great challenges and to endure adversity. In time, my mother decided that she and we three youngest children would carry on alone, with the tending of the farm. Our age and inexperience seemed of little consequence to her decision. My sister, Karen, was then 17; my brother John, 15; and I was 8. My oldest brother, Forest, who had a young family of his own to care for, had worked the farm for a time right after our father's death. But the drought that year caused the fields and pastures to dry up, and there was little income from the land. He was forced to turn to another career, and we carried on alone.

Many years later I asked my mother why she had decided to stay, why she had decided to continue farming, in the face of such difficult odds. "You were a teacher," I said. "Why didn't you choose to make a living that way?" .

Mom simply shrugged. "I thought farming would be the best way we could make a living," she replied. I knew Mom's definition of making a living included sending her kids to college. I had asked the question out of a momentary but passing suspicion that our lives might have been easier and simpler had she decided to teach rather than farm. But I believe Mom saw opportunities in agriculture then—as indeed there were. It was the 1960s. Farm-production and farm-family-living costs were still fairly low compared to the prices farmers received for their products, such as wheat, barley, pork, milk, and beef.

Variable weather, of course, was the great uncertainty my mother would have to face each year, just as farmers of the prairies have done since the first plow sliced a furrow in the soil of the Northern Plains. Rainy spells and time of droughts take turns besetting the Plains, in no predictable order. If the early rains come too hard, too often, they wash away farmers' freshly planted seeds. On the other hand, heavy rains followed by hot, dry weather often bake the top of the soil into a hard crust, which tiny seedlings cannot push through. When droughts come, plants struggle to grow, and yields are small. Grasshoppers, hail, and plant diseases all take their toll, too, on crops and pastures. In short, some years are boom; some years are bust for farmers and ranchers of the Northern Plains.

Nevertheless, Mom decided to gamble on farming. And so, despite our inexperience as farmers, we three children leaned into the harness of responsibilities, pulling the load of the farmwork as a team. At 15, my brother John took over the job of growing the crops and keeping the farm machinery running. Besides the 400 acres that my father and mother owned, they rented two additional quarters of land, or 320 acres. My mother continued to rent this extra land for a few years after the death of my father. My sister helped my brother do the farmwork; in spring they planted the fields together, each driving a tractor pulling a plow with a seed-drill attached behind. Every morning and evening Mom, John, and Karen milked the cows.

My mother managed the work of the farm more by determination than careful planning. It seems we often found ourselves facing situations that were nearly out of control. Mom decided, for instance, that we should add pigs to the farm. At her bidding, Karen and John put up a spacious woven-wire pen beneath the box elder trees in the old tree shelterbelt on the west side of the barnyard. Several sows lived there, and they and their offspring soon became artists at escaping from the enclosure by rooting away the soil from underneath the wire. Each escape sent Karen and John on a wild pig chase around the yard.

Calamity sometimes accompanied the birth of piglets. Once a sow had a litter of pigs in winter, but she gave no milk to feed her babies.

Determined to save the piglets, Mom moved them into the house, setting up a makeshift, cardboard pen on the dining-room floor. She fed the starving baby pigs cow's milk from a baby's bottle. As the piglets gained strength, they crashed down their cardboard corral and scattered their bed of newspaper all across the floor. The next most logical pen, my mother decided, was the bathtub, because its sides afforded more formidable barriers for the energetic little animals. I recall studying the tub and its piglet-tenants, in all their messy glory, wondering just how long one would have to endure this time of going without a bathtub for the sake of the baby pigs.

Handling cattle held special challenges, too. Once, we needed to treat a sick cow in a pasture a long way from home. Mom had rented my grandparents' rangeland, which was 10 miles away from our farm. We hauled the cattle to the pasture with a two-ton truck, which had a box with a deck four feet off the ground. Since there were no working corrals or unloading chutes on the pasture, unloading the cattle from the truck safely was a problem. But John and Karen came up with a plan: Using hand shovels, they dug a recessed space into the side of a hill. They could then back the truck up, so that its rear wheels fit into the space, allowing the box to nearly touch the ground on the side of the hill. When the cattle came out of the truck, they had to jump down only about a foot to reach ground level. The arrangement let us unload cattle easily at the pasture. We didn't plan on ever having to load them back into the truck since we were able to herd them back home in the fall on horseback.

But one year, after we had hauled the cattle to pasture, one of the cows got sick and needed to be treated. The only option was to haul her home, since we had no corrals at the pasture. But neither did we have a way of corraling the cow in order to load her into the truck. And though the cow was growing thin and obviously looked sick, she was still far from placid. Yet, we were innocent believers. We set out to capture the cow by sheer determination—and God's help for the helpless.

A PRAYER FOR THE PRAIRIE

My brother John backed the truck up into the dugout in the side of the hill and opened the narrow gate into the box. Then we three set off across the hills looking for the sick cow. We believed we could simply chase her into the truck without the aid of corrals, fence panels, or any other barriers. When we found the herd, we cut the sick cow out and herded her toward the truck. As we neared it, however, the cow tried to veer away from the hulking object, which sat glaring and gleaming in the middle of the bare-naked prairie like a great metal beetle burrowing into the bald hill. Within a hundred yards of the truck, the cow spooked completely. She stuck her tail out and ducked away from the truck, circling around us, galloping full tilt the half a mile back to her herdmates.

We took off in full chase, our legs pumping wildly up the hills and over the crests. I recall how my churning limbs could barely keep up with the momentum of my body going downhill, giving the sensation of being in a free fall. The thorny stems of wild rose bushes grabbed at the skin beneath my bluejeans as I flailed through the thickets growing at the bases of hills. Each time we retrieved the cow from the herd and chased her back to the truck, she spooked and escaped. Back and forth we chased her, till my chest seemed on fire and my legs felt as tottery and flimsy as strips of cotton. Then, as I ran, a strange thing happened. My wind came back, and my muscles strengthened, making my stride once again fleet and sure. Led by the hand of God, it seems, the cow finally yielded, walking willingly through the narrow opening of the truck box. I asked my mother later, about the miraculous return of my breath and strength. She said I had simply caught my "second wind."

And so it was that farm life taught us that success could usually be achieved by pushing past exhaustion, beyond the point of seeming impossibility. When I was 12, for instance, it seemed of little consequence to me to clean the dairy barn in winter using only a small wheelbarrow. During weekdays Karen and John were away at college, leaving Mom and me to tend the cattle alone. We usually cleaned the barn by pitching the manure from the gutter into a manure spreader. We used a tractor to pull the spreader to the field. By setting a lever on the spreader, a chain began rotating in the bed of the spreader, unloading the manure automatically.

But sometimes there was too much snow to drive the tractor in the field. That's when I would clean the barn with a wheelbarrow, setting to the task after getting off the schoolbus in the afternoons. Fourteen cows stood in the barn all night and most of the day. I scraped straw and manure from the cement platform where they stood and from the deep gutter running the length of the barn. I pitched the manure into the wheelbarrow and wheeled it out of the barn, over the crests of snowdrifts hardened by the wind, following a trail I had made around the barn to the manure pile. After eight or so trips the barn was clean.

One afternoon, Mom had not yet returned from a business appointment by the time I got home from school. The dairy barn's heavy back barn door was frozen shut, and I couldn't open it alone. This meant I wasn't able to let the cows out for water. So I cleaned the barn with the cows still standing on the platform, and then I began watering them with five-gallon buckets, lugging the water by hand from the well 30 feet from the barn. I felt weary that night but triumphant because I had not let a small obstacle like a stuck barn door derail me from my chores. But most importantly, I had done the extra work because I felt needed, significant. My mother was surprised and grateful, when she returned later in the afternoon, to find that so much had already been done.

As time passed, the farm prospered. We had, in the years since my father's death, reduced the amount of land we farmed so that we were responsible only for the 400 acres Mom owned and an additional 68 acres of pastureland she had bought, plus a portion of my grandparents' pasture. But Mom had expanded her dairy herd to 30 head, and this modest expansion strengthened the farm. By this time—the late 1960s—greater prosperity was evident on many other farms in our community. Neighbors expanded their dairy herds, too, erecting spacious barns and tall feed silos whose gleaming metal tops became landmarks looming up from the horizon. It was a time when a farm formed a hub for a family's labor and commerce. The average prices farmers earned for their milk, grain, beef, and pork paid them a good income for their labor and management ingenuity. Indeed, many families could earn a fair livelihood from farming.

The changes on our farm were significant by the late 1960s and early 1970s. My brother John had long since demolished the old A-frame barn that had once been the center of the farmyard. The old barn was replaced by a flat dairy barn and later on, a modernized three-stall milking parlor in which the cows stood on an elevated platform to be milked. A glass pipeline carried the milk from the milkers into an anteroom, where the milk emptied into a bulk milk cooler. A large, new steel barn provided shelter for the cows at night and in bad weather. We had the equipment we needed to conveniently care for the cattle—a new tractor, a new baler, a new hay mower, a new pickup and by the early 1970s, a second new pickup along with a new horse trailer. After my brother and sister graduated from college, my mother and I worked alone together for nearly eight years, tending the cattle but renting the farmland out.

The farm became the only form of livelihood that I knew. Still, it was to me much more than a place of enterprise. Indeed, the work of tending cattle, fences, and fields held no economic value to me. I did the work because it was my life. Like a squirrel compelled to gather and stash its food, I was compelled to stretch my muscles tightening fence wires, digging postholes, slinging bales, pitching manure; compelled to feel the wind and sun on my face; compelled to breath in air carrying the sweet fragrance of prairie roses in summer and the pungent scent of farmers burning stubble fields in fall.

If I were an artist painting the face of the mythical Mother Nature reigning over the Northern Plains, I would use colors and brush strokes portraying stunning beauty, ugliness, triumph, and tragedy. Her countenance seems fixed in the hearts of those who have spent their sweat toiling in her gardens. Her energy is the epicenter of emotion for those who have clung to her skirts as children. Indeed, her expressions are the barometers of my life. I am whole and at peace when I see the Big Dipper shining down over the cottonwoods to the north, or when Orion stands straight up in the southern sky at bedtime, signaling the nearness of winter's end. Nature's events are my emotional signposts, a web of past experiences wrapping me to her bosom in a grip defining my reality.

It was so for my mother also. Her senses and emotions too were tied to the land, to the sky, and to the wind. That connection may have had the greatest influence on her decision so many long years before to carry on farming. No other form of livelihood could have enshrouded her with the emotional security she needed. Living amidst God's creation is to be surrounded continually by visibile, audible, and tactile evidence of His Presence. There is comfort in this.

The last two months of my mother's life she spent partially paralyzed, living in a care center in a town 20 miles from the farm she loved so dearly. One day after I had pushed her wheelchair outside so we could feel the sun and breeze on our faces, Mom asked, "Did you see how beautiful the sunset was last night?" I said, yes, I had seen its brilliant display of orange and bronze light. She fell silent for a spell, her eyes searching the western sky. Finally she spoke: "I was thinking that if you saw the sunset at the same time as I did, it would be a way we could communicate with each other."

* * *

Now, I stand atop my Prayer Hill, watching the sun's sinking rays. I remember my mother's words, and I wonder: Do God's thoughts permeate the sunset? If I watch intently and listen carefully, can I hear them? Will He reveal His words to me if I search for His wisdom humbly and earnestly? On days when my spirit is filled with peace, I do not have to ask such a question. I know the answer is yes. But on this evening I am deeply troubled, and I wonder how long God will keep silent concerning this matter weighing so heavily so often:

The prosperous years of farming, which I recall from my youth, are long gone. Our family farm is a testament. The milking parlor sits empty, paint peeling from its walls. The flat dairy barn, which I cleaned with a wheelbarrow as a youngster, stands now like an old horse, its back weak and bowed. The shingles on the roof of our hulking old house are gray and loose. These external deficiencies on our farm signal the depth of the financial difficulties besetting a host of other family farmers. The prices farmers receive for the most common types of crops and livestock hardly pay for the costs incurred in producing these crops. Prices for grain, for instance, are very nearly at the same level as they were 25 years ago. By contrast, farmers' costs have doubled or quadrupled since the 1970s. As a result, farm newspapers have overflowed with notices of family-farm auctions.

Longtime farmer-neighbors from over the hill to the east of us have left, forced by tight finances to sell. Just kitty-corner from our farm to the northeast, other longtime neighbors with a farming heritage three generations deep and a debt they were unable to pay were sold out by lenders. Friends with a 20-year vision of making a living from the land now work in town. Other friends' eyes show disheartenment from years of struggling against the forces afflicting agriculture.

Still, John and I have not given up. We are farmers by blood. Can a bird dog stop hunting? Can a singer stop singing? Can a painter stop painting? Often, when I look at my Canadian-bred husband, I see a man who is conformed to his Mennonite farming heritage by deep sinews of tradition and skills that have their origins in generations of collective experience: the adroit turn of a garden spade, reading the soil trickling through the hand, diagnosing the illness of an uncomfortable cow. My husband came with me to this farm a little more than a decade ago. We came with great hope, hope for nurturing the land, tilling the soil profitably and filling the pastures with thriving livestock. But the difficulties have taxed our hope nearly to its death. Year after year, we have barely survived financially.

Yet our dream lingers, and we are able to continue farming by God's grace. Each winter germinates new ideas, new alternatives, new strategies, new ways of farming that may bring financial sustainability. I long for an enduring life on the land, days filled with using my hands and body to do the good and useful work that causes sleek-sided calves to grow into robust yearlings, the work that will entice plants to spring from the earth and produce healthy food—food for which we are paid a fair price. It is a longing I feel literally as an internal moving, much like the inner pulling I recall from my childhood the first time I recognized the beauty of a prairie rose.

I truly saw the exquisiteness of the prairie rose for the first time the year I turned 10. It was a still, sultry afternoon in late July, and I was riding my horse, Buck. I must have passed wild roses numerous times in my field forays on Buck. But on this particular day a prairie rose fixed its vision in my mind with the permanence of a painting hung in a gallery. The single, pink flower crowned a tiny shrub, barely a foot high, growing in drought-browned grass along the trail just north of the farmstead. I recall how the sight of the simple flower with its tiny center of yellow stamens surrounded by pastel petals filled me with a fascination—and a mysterious yearning. I slid off of Buck's back and leaned down to inspect the flower. In the still air, the rose's sweet scent hung close about me, incense for a sacred moment. Maybe it was a moment of strengthening, for it became a vision intertwining itself with the flowers and thorns of the dream growing inside of me—a yearning, longing pulling to live and work always with soil and animals under the arching freedom of God's wide-open skies.

On some days now, a lifetime later, I see this vision slowly coming to pass. Yet on other days I see it slipping farther and farther into oblivion. This day that I stand atop my Prayer Hill is a day when hope is distant. It feels as though my husband, John, and I cannot possibly find our "second wind" and that we are bound to lose this gamble called farming, a gamble with a jackpot that seemingly cannot be corralled. It feels as though we will never be able to wrangle a fair living from the prices the marketplace pays for our products. It seems sure we are bound to lose this way of life that has been bred into our bones for generations. It seems we are among but a remnant of an old and dying breed—family farmers who make their living growing food, but who do it because they cannot help themselves, because they are, as another woman farmer puts it, "like the spruce trees" planted by her grandmother—growing where they are rooted.

But are we as tough as those spruce trees? Are John and I indeed as sturdy and enduring as the volunteer plants thriving on the Big Hill? Do we have the hardiness, ingenuity, and luck required to survive these harsh economic winds blowing across the face of agriculture?

With these unanswered questions, I stand before My Father on my Prayer Hill. The setting sun is a golden orb rimmed in ruby, bathing the horizon in rose-tinted light. The radiant scene stirs in my mind these words from the biblical prophet Habakkuk:

"I will take my stand to watch, and station myself on the tower, and look forth to see what he will say to me, and what I will answer concerning my complaint. And the Lord answered me:

" 'Write the vision; make it plain upon tablets, so he may run who reads it. For still the vision awaits its time; it hastens to the end—it will not lie. If it seem slow, wait for it; it will surely come, it will not delay. Behold, he whose soul is not upright in him shall fail, but the righteous shall live by his faith.' "

The words are gentle goads, prodding me to see what yet remains unseen, to cast my faith ahead of fact. And so, from the ashes of my hope I reconstruct again our vision, and in my mind's eye it regains its shape until I see it clearly once more: A farm that is a garden. The fields spread out before me, green and healthy, burgeoning with a variety of crops—wheat, barley, oats, lentils, peas, alfalfa, grass, and sweet clover. The soil is rich and mellow, filled with root and residue particles and the activity of earthworms and other soil life. Tree shelterbelts crisscross the land, and every 60 acres has a water spot. The wetlands are ringed by volunteer trees, and birds abound so that insects are in check. Deer take shelter under the trees; waterfowl live in the wetlands, and pheasants, partridge, and sharp-tailed grouse thrive amid the farm's diverse vegetation. The pastures are filled with grass and romping calves and lambs.

Below me, to the southwest, the buildings of the farmstead are healed, painted, and once again they stand straight and strong. I scan the horizon all around and see, in my mind's eye, farms where other families nurture their land and reap bountiful harvests that pay them for their labor. I see my husband and me working beside each other, supporting each other, becoming everything God envisioned us to become when He first formed us. I see us crafting a place of healing, peace, and prosperity from this farm.

But when I blink, a shadow of doubt once more clouds my sight, and discouragement settles again upon my shoulders. Peering helplessly into the sunset, I pray: "If I have loved this life too much—so much that I have lost sight of Your truth, then tear up my roots and plant me somewhere else."

But I sense no reply, only the peaceful, healing silence of nature's sounds—crickets chirping and the rustling of the breeze through the clover.

And so I set my face to the west and walk down the hill, my resolve once more fixed on the work of helping my husband to build a flourishing garden from a faltering farm.

AN ECONOMY
OF THE HEART
2001

It is late afternoon when I stroll through the cow herd. This is early February, and John has just unrolled a big, round bale of hay for the cows to eat. He's gone again, off to fetch yet another bale from the far corner of the Eighty, a field north of the farmstead. It's a quiet and reflective affair, this walking among the cows in winter. There is no music in the air on this wind-still day since the songbirds of summer are long gone, sequestering themselves in warmer abodes of more southern climes, where they wait for spring to wash over the North. Then they will come back in droves to their favorite haunts amid pastures, potholes, and shelterbelts. The cold of a North Dakota winter silences too the crickets and grasshoppers, whose sawing and clacking in summer cover the ground with a blanket of soft, constant sound.

Now, with the temperature hovering at 10 degrees above zero, the hard snow crunches under the cows' hooves as they jostle each other, searching for the choicest morsels of hay. The muffled rustling of their chewing stirs in me a comforting familiarity, a sense that all is well. I have come here, among the cows, to seek solace from the day's pressures.

As I edge around them, studying each one, I feel lighter, more joyful, even though barely an hour ago I was yelling at the top of my lungs at these creatures. They had escaped out of an open gate and had come frolicking past the house on the side opposite my upstairs office. A sound akin to distant thunder caught my attention, and when I looked outside, I saw them: tails up, gleefully romping along the lilac hedge. Quickly donning coat and boots, I dashed outside and—with much yelling and arm waving—managed to herd them back into the corral through another open gate.

That small hardship is now forgotten. I have come to the cows in search of hope. I am seeking signs of spring, and I am not disappointed. In front of me stands a handsome red-roan cow, who studies me with placid eyes. Her name is Daisy, and though she is still three months from giving birth to her calf, her well-rounded belly promises to deliver a good-sized baby in mid-May. A favorite of mine, this cow is a stocky version of the docile Milking Shorthorn cattle of my youth. Indeed, Daisy's unborn calf is sired by a son of a grand old Milking Shorthorn bull by the name of Korncrest Pacesetter, a popular sire among Shorthorn breeders 25 years ago. In my youth I artificially inseminated many of my mother's dairy cows to Pacesetter.

I move toward a different clutch of cows and find Nora. Strong and deep-bodied, this old red-and-white cow is herself a straightbred Milking Shorthorn. Thinking of her coming calf makes me feel like a kid again, full of joyful expectancy. We artificially inseminated Nora to old Korncrest Pacesetter himself. Though the old bull's frozen semen is no longer available commercially, John and I were able to buy two doses of it last summer from a Milking Shorthorn breeder in Minnesota. We view the infusion of Pacesetter's blood into our herd to be an important stepping stone to our goal of building a herd of cows that are heavy milking but easy fleshing—cows that will thrive on the grasses and legumes growing so abundantly on our farm. The coming birth of the calves—with their sleek, seal-like hides, innocent eyes, and wild races around the pasture—is to me as a distant pool of shimmering water is to a desert traveler.

Presently I hear muffled clopping and a dull, scraping sound coming from the north. I turn in time to see John driving his team of big, grey horses through the north gateway to the pasture. The team of Percheron geldings, Pete and Skeet, pull a round, 1,000-pound bale of hay cabled onto a short-bodied and low, plank-and-steel deck on runners. A broad, three-foot deep bank of wind-hardened snow blocks the gateway. It would stop even a newfangled front-wheel-assist tractor dead in its tracks. But the big drift hardly causes Pete and Skeet to break stride. They lug their load straight over the top of the bank, through the gateway and down the other side.

I stand still, watching, listening, as John and his horse-partners pull the bale to the far end of the cow herd. The clip-clop of hooves and swishing of the sled's runners on snow are subdued sounds as from a dream. I marvel at how calmly Pete and Skeet handle their work, noses gracefully tucked as they yield to the bit, heads and tails steady.

"Whoa!" John commands, and the horses stop near the cows. He dallies the lines around a brace at the front of the sled. Pete and Skeet stand patiently then while John releases the bale from the cable and unrolls it by hand for the cows to eat.

This way of feeding the herd is silent, unobtrusive. The cattle are hardly disrupted by the quiet presence of the big horses. It seems that John, too, works in a steadier, calmer rhythm than he did before, when he fed the cows with a tractor—as nearly every farmer or rancher in our community does. Folks driving by on the road, seeing this performance of John and his horses, must think him old-fashioned. Yet I consider him ahead of his time, an engineer of sorts, adapting an old technology to modern needs. He designed this horse-drawn bale hauler himself, welding the braces at the front and attaching the crank that loosens or tightens the cable.

After John rolls out the bale for the cows, he steps back on the sled and undallies the lines from the crosspiece. "Step!" he commands, and Pete and Skeet walk ahead, angling to where I stand. Opposite me they stop, and John says: "Do you want to go along to get another bale?" Of course I do. I step on the sled, and John drives the team around the herd and toward the open gate. Just outside the opening the team must make a hard left turn. "Haw, Pete," says John, flicking the left line, and the biggest grey horse sidesteps to the left, followed a half step later by Skeet. These commands of John's—haw for left and gee for right—are indeed remnants of an old, nearly forgotten language, one spoken generations ago by teamsters talking to their horses and oxen.

Though I have worked with saddle horses most of my life, I am an outsider to this rapport between the teamster and his team. I have held the team's lines in my hands but once, and I habitually forget that haw is for left and gee is for right. Lack of skill isn't the only thing blocking my entrance into this special union between horse and man. The 16-hand, 1,800-pound horses intimidate me. They are obedient, but they are also energetic. It's not unusual for Pete to become startled, bunch his body like a folded accordian and try to break out into a canter. Yet John can calm him with a single word.

I feel left out somehow—or maybe left behind. I sense I must scramble to catch up with John as he delves farther and farther back into agricultural technology for the sources of power that we can afford and that are as regenerative as possible. The technology of teamstering predates me. I was a child when my mother sold my father's big horses soon after his death in 1960. The closest I came to driving them was when my dad set me on top of one to go for a short ride. I clung to the hames jutting up from the horse's collar as Dad drove his quiet team through a gate.

Now, it's my husband's hands that pick up the reins. It's my husband's voice that speaks in undertones to his team, and soon Pete and Skeet are long-trotting down the side of the driveway, heading for a field to pick up a big, round bale of straw for bedding for the cows. The ground flashes by; the cold breeze bites my face, and the trepidations of the day fall away. There is a sacred sensuousness in this moment: Ahead of us, the muscles of the horses' heavy hindquarters rise and fall in the graceful, hypnotic rhythm of their stride. The scent of their light sweat is strangely invigorating. It wafts back to us on the rivulets of the breeze, a sweetish yet acrid smell conjuring hazy visions of county fairs, meadows of freshly cut grass, and handfuls of moist, tilled earth. Beside me, my husband stands relaxed, attention focused on the team, balancing his work-hardened body in counterpoint to shifts in the sled's movement.

In this moment we glide along at the same pace, riding lightly, almost stealthily on the surface of the earth, the silence broken only by the rhythmic, muffled clopping of horses' hooves on hard-packed snow. Though I indeed feel that I am an outsider to this special union John has with his team, nevertheless I feel intimately joined to him in the moment. I know that we are writing on the same page of life's book. As I study his bearded face, I am thankful that John Nickel is my husband. I am grateful that our burning passions are one. We are yoked together by a common yearning, driven by a unity of spirit. Like the neckyoke and evener binding Pete and Skeet into a team, our unity keeps us pulling in the same direction. Late in life, my mother, once a teamster herself, wrote about the early years of her marriage, during the 1930s: "Life was a challenge, and we worked as a good team of horses pulling together. Sights always forward to the building of a home and a family."

John and I have our sights set on the building of a farm. Yet it is an aspiration much more complex, more multifaceted than such a statement tells. Indeed, the farm may simply be a product of our broader aim: to live and provide for our needs in simple ways bound by nature's cycles; to have souls of faith, hope, and love; to be numbered among God's tools.

On the way home from the field, with the straw bale in tow, John stops at the main road, so that I can step down from the sled and resume my afternoon walk. I want to walk hard for at least two miles, stretching my legs and getting my circulation pumping again, to counter the stress and fatigue I often feel. I am a free-lance agricultural writer, and though it is an occupation that is home based and surely has idylic benefits, it is nevertheless one cut from the corporate cloth. It's not uncommon for me to put in 10- and 12-hour days behind a desk and computer for six days a week—sometimes seven, particularly in winter. Occasionally I go on 24-hour writing binges to bail myself out of tight deadlines. In many ways, I am simply a word machine.

In this way my commercialized writing frequently rides the coattails of corporate profits in order to provide an economic rudder for our small farm. Of course, as a free-lancer, I am free to choose the weight of my workload. I choose it to be heavy, since my work is part of the economic plan that keeps us farming.

John's development of low-cost farming techniques comprises another prong to our survival strategy. The sled and team exemplify a tool and a power source springing from John's searching and striving for ways to operate the farm without depending so heavily on fuel, expensive machinery, and other costly inputs. To revamp the hay sled, which was given to us as a castaway, John invested only $70.

Our team, however, did cost $3,500 and, indeed, a similar investment might purchase a serviceable chore tractor of 20 to 30 years in age. But it would take a new tractor with bi-directional traction to rival the horses' ability to navigate deep snow, and such tractors cost in the neighborhood of $90,000. Moreover, the horses' labor requires no daily out-of-pocket cash. Though Pete and Skeet hauled 570 round bales and traveled about 1,250 miles over the course of three winter months, the easy-keeping horses ate only hay throughout the winter—hay we did not have to purchase because we grew it on our farm last summer. By contrast, a tractor requires daily infusions of cash in the form of purchased fuel.

The winter work of John and his horse-partners indeed tells a success story of agricultural sustainability. But our small farm is still far from being self-supporting. Time and infusions of working capital are needed before all the pieces of the puzzle can slip into place. So . . . while John spends his days working on farm projects, I work at the computer. In that regard, our lives run a track similar to a host of other farm couples, where wives work away from home, as well as some farm husbands. Many small and mid-size family farmers have taken jobs off the farm—in addition to farming—to shore up the shortfalls in actual net income caused by low commodity prices and high input costs.

Given today's economic climate for agriculture and the stage of the financial development of our farm, the ingenuity and work required for us to earn enough money to cover expenses causes an unrelenting pressure. But for John and me, the rewards lie in the way of life. Farming is much more to us than just a business; indeed, it is something of a calling, just as it is for many other family farmers.

But in the course of my work, I occasionally interview agribusiness professionals who pointedly differentiate between farmers who treat farming "as a business" and those who treat it as a way of life. They hold the business-minded farmers in esteem and seem to glance askew at those who view farming as a way of life. The thread of this thinking—that farming should be viewed strictly as a business—is put upon us from numerous directions. Indeed, it has been woven into our own lives for several generations, since it has in fact been a function of necessity. As a farm partner, I have sat at the kitchen table across from my husband, figuring and refiguring the potential costs and income of raising cattle, hogs, and sheep. The handwriting on the wall speaks clearly: Without a profit there is no livelihood to be made from the farm.

Yet if John and I had treated our own farming venture strictly as a business from the start, we would probably not be farming now. We would have quit long before the time when our cupboards went bare; long before the time we became so economically paralyzed we could do nothing but stay. Some may even contend had we viewed farming and ranching solely as a business, we never should have returned to this small family farm in the first place. A thread of truth runs through each of these notions.

Farming is surely a business in the sense that where it generates costs and debts, these must be paid. A farm should provide, too, for the food, health, clothing, and shelter needed by the people who live and work on its land.

Yet there is more, so much more than money driving this life. When joy is born of warm chinook breezes, the meadowlark's song in spring, green threads of oats and alfalfa seedlings peeping through the soil, and a walk with my husband when the distant hills appear as a mirage against the skyline, what role does money play in all this? Indeed, money is needful. But a 90-some elder who still works as a peddler of junked-out farm machinery asks in church one day, "How much is enough?"

As John and I struggle up from the ashes of a financial burn down, I often catch myself considering just that question: How much is enough? Should we strive for a new car, or a 10-year-old car? A new, or a used stove? A tractor with a cab, or a team of willing horses?

What track do you follow when love, joy, and faith beckon from a distant meadow, calling you to a useful work you love, but a shortage of money—or some other stubborn obstacle—appears as a boulder blocking your path?

The more often I ask these questions, the more often I find myself seeking prosperity in odd places. A centerpiece for my thinking is the biblical story of the half-shekel tax and the fish. The story tells that Jesus needed to pay a tax, so with this command he sent his disciple Peter to fish in the sea: "Take the first fish that comes up, and when you open its mouth, you will find a shekel ... ."

Jesus' simple, seemingly nonsensical instruction speaks to me of a true and enduring prosperity transcending money, transcending human reason. It is God's prosperity; it is improbable; it makes the impossible possible. I long for it to permeate our lives and spill over into the fields of this farm. Indeed, often I do see it seeping into the fringes. I get glimpses of such a prosperity when we happen upon duck nests during pasture walks, when handfuls of soil trickle through our fingers in fat, healthy crumbs rather than fine, sand-like particles—and when our best cows give birth to fine heifer calves, calves that will go on to become productive young cows.

Perhaps because I am so thankful for food, I get the most striking impressions of prosperity when I work in our garden. I was raised to view gardening as an antiquated millstone to economic progressiveness. "You can't make money raising a garden!" my mother would exclaim, striding off to the milking parlor, built in 1968, when I was 15. The convenient parlor let us expand our dairy herd from 14 head to a little more than 30. The parlor was designed so that the cows walked up onto a platform to be milked. The platform was at waist height for the milkers, and we could milk three cows at once. There was no need to lift the heavy milking machines, as we once did, since hoses carried the milk from the suction cups into an overhead pipelines, which carried the milk into a refrigerated bulk tank.

Since the cows spent the winter free-ranging in the corral and a large open barn, there was no need to clean manure from the gutter of the old stanchion barn, which had now been converted into a barn for rearing calves. Still, the cement-floor holding area, where the cows waited their turn to walk up the four steps into the parlor, had to be scraped by hand of manure daily. And all of the elaborate milking equipment and hoses and pipelines required much cleaning to meet the requirements of inspectors who now visited our farm periodically to ensure we produced milk according to healthful standards. The work of dairying seemed to leave no time for gardening, and so I grew up eating food purchased from the store.

As an adult, I shunned serious gardening with disdain, even after John and I came to North Dakota to tend the farm where I was raised. I was sure that we did a better job of surviving by spending as much time as possible earning off-the-farm incomes to buy necessities such as groceries, rather than spending our hard-pressed time to grow our own food.

But I scrimped on groceries to save money. Then one winter there was no money, and I scrimped even more, not even recognizing that we were growing more and more tired in both body and spirit. That winter my sister, Karen, shared the bounty from her large garden: carrots, potatoes, cabbage, and squash. I began to see an absurdity in our situation: Farmers with no food? What nonsense! Having access, as we did, to rich farmland, the acquisition of food should not demand a monetary exchange, I reasoned. The exchange required should be one of human energy. We determined that our food should result from a direct partnership between us and the soil we tend.

When we began to take it seriously, gardening evolved for us into a mysterious yet obvious fish in the sea. Now our garden represents an integral part of our lives: a year's supply of diverse vegetables, health. It is the fuel that sparks our creativity; it supplies the energy we need when we walk somewhere on this 468-acre farm, which we do often in the course of a day's work. The garden helps to supply the fuel we need to perform a growing assortment of hand-powered tasks. The garden insulates our food supply from the economic vicissitudes of the world, at the same time seeming to contribute, along with largely home-produced meat and some dairy products, to greater energy, fewer aches and pains, and a need for fewer and fewer pills.

To do all this, our garden demands only a small input of cash. Fertility is supplied by natural soil processes, helped along by some composted manure or legumes. We control weeds by hand. Garden seed is our only expense, simply because we are not yet organized enough . . . or not yet skillful enough . . . or possibly not yet freed enough emotionally from our economic treadmill, to take the time to add another layer of prosperity to the garden enterprise by saving our own seeds.

Yet, mysteriously, a garden provides much more than physical sustenance. Functioning like a miniature farm, a garden is a source of hope and inspiration, a bounty of new beginnings. Not long after I took up serious gardening in my early 40s, I wrote in a newspaper column: "A garden is a place that embraces you once you step inside its boundaries. It's a society all its own, with its own unique industry. The radishes clamor to be picked; the carrots plead to be thinned; and the cabbages call for me to come and simply admire their progress, while the beans stand like calm sentinels, waiting for a final inspection. I used to thumb my nose at gardening. It was, I contended, an activity that simply got in the way of everything else that needed doing in life—like making a living. And once a day was spent in the pursuit of that, who would want to expend additional energy hoeing and picking weeds?

"But I didn't know, then, about the counsel of the bean. I didn't know that one day, in a garden, I would discover a semblance of tranquility and some sense of the natural order of life."

How can any yardsticks of economic value measure the vastness of such spiritual benefits? For these are woven into the holistic, intricate pattern of God's prosperity, a boundless, freeing force loosed in heaven. By contrast, our economics of profit and loss seem heavy, materialistic bodies chained to earth by our language and thoughts of lack, through our seemingly perpetual need for more of everything.

Seeking God's prosperity in our lives and on our farm is an unfolding mystery to me: What we view as success, God may view as failure; while what we view as failure, may be His success. Trying to live out the mystery has demanded endurance and sometimes blind trust, trust to continue walking forward even though going forward means moving closer to the center of a storm of difficulty . . . such as what came to us in the mid-1990s.

During that period cattle sales comprised the lion's share of our income, but prices spiraled downward, eliminating profits. At the time, most of the money required to run the farm came from bank loans, which had to be repaid annually.

Then came the winter of 1996-97. One blizzard after another hammered the Dakotas with high winds, heavy snow, and below-zero temperatures. Some roads were blocked for days and farmsteads crippled. Thousands of cattle died that winter in South and North Dakota as a result of the blizzards.

At the time, John and I lived on a small farmstead we had purchased. It was 10 miles from our main family farm, where my elderly mother lived in the farmhouse. Because of the harsh weather and because snowdrifts blocked the roads so often that driving back and forth between the two places became impossible some days, John left our home in January to live at the main farm, where he could tend the cattle full time. I continued living at our own small farmstead, and my mother came to live with me there for several weeks before traveling to Washington to spend the rest of the winter with my brother and his family.

It was good that my mother spent much of the winter in Washington. Most of the time I was snow-locked at our isolated farmhouse, with no vehicle, our driveway often plugged with heavy snowdrifts banked up by the frequent high winds.

During one of these snow-locked spells I ran low on heating fuel for the house. My sister brought 10-gallon pails of diesel fuel in a pickup to the corner below our long driveway. I walked down to meet her, and we pulled the pails on a sled nearly a mile back to our farmhouse. During this time I worked practically nonstop at my computer, forcing out words that would earn cash, taking time only to eat, sleep, and go for walks on days when the wind was not howling. But I could not work hard enough to fill the void in cash left by that winter's crashing cattle prices.

My husband's days were trying, too. At the main farm the tractor he had been using to feed hay to the cattle stood at the end of the driveway, suffering from a breakdown too costly for us to repair. Luckily, we had a team of young black mares on loan from a friend, and John used the team to feed hay to the cattle. But the mares, though willing to work hard, were not trustworthy. They occasionally ran away with the hay sled when John stepped off to open or shut gates. During one runaway they tore down a section of fence. On another the mares ran on either side of a heavy brace wire angling into the ground from the top of a telephone pole. One of the mares ended up partly dangling from the wire, held there by the crosspieces of her harness, still hitched to the other mare.

During one blizzard John severed the fleshy end of a finger nearly completely off while moving a fence panel. Even if he had wanted to see a doctor about the finger, he could not have traveled to one because the road to town was blocked by drifted snow. Since the fingertip was still attached by skin on one side of the finger, John decided to save it. Stuffing snow on his head under his woolen stocking cap to keep from fainting, he repositioned the severed fingertip in its rightful place. Then he hurried to the house and slathered the wounded finger with medicinal honey salve and bandaged it. It eventually healed soundly, with only a slight appearance of crookedness.

But healing was a long way off for my mental state. Our economic paralysis seeped into my mind that winter, blocking any view of the future, and indeed, any sense of an alternate livelihood. Our exhausting work seemed as fruitless as tossing pebbles into the ocean to make waves. I began to feel numb, moving through my days as through a haze. One afternoon, too paralyzed to write, I leaned heavily on the kitchen counter, staring out the window at the snow-covered hills beyond our house. In my mind's eye, the scene was transfigured, obliterated by a black wall. John and I stood before the wall, hand in hand. My gut felt frozen, my chest too heavy to breathe. I thought: "We cannot get past this wall. The only way past it is to go around. Yet it seems too huge to get around."

Then I noticed a rippling in the surface of the "wall," as thin cloth ripples in the breeze. The thought came to me that the black, ominous wall was simply a sham. I saw too that as John and I moved toward, it receded, never fading from sight, yet always receding as we pressed on, walking into it. I drew courage from the insight; it was an answer to prayer. I resolved to keep walking forward into the farming life we had chosen, though economically it seemed to make no sense.

AN ECONOMY OF THE HEART

* * *

My father and mother faced a similar critical economic period in their careers as farmers. They started farming in the spring of 1936, just short of a year after their marriage. With the end of the Depression still not in sight, they couldn't have picked a more difficult time to begin. After several months of searching for farms to rent, they found a 160-acre homestead. The rent for the year was $100, which Mom saved from her income as a teacher in one-room rural schools. Her wage had been $45 a month.

The livestock they brought to their little farm included a cow, two pigs, two saddle horses, and 20 chickens they bought at an auction sale for $1 each. Mom's father gave them the pigs—a sow and a boar—and Dad's father gave them the cow as well as a rusty old cream separator destined for the junk heap. Selling cream from that one cow kept my folks supplied with groceries until the chickens began laying eggs later that spring, eggs to sell in town. My mother's father gave them 20 bushels of wheat seed to plant. Dad seeded some corn, too, but that summer it was so dry the corn seed didn't germinate until September, after a little rain came. My folks pulled the scraggly corn plants by hand in October and fed them to the cow.

The wheat crop yielded eight bushels, not even enough for seed for the following spring. The cow and horses ate no grain, and even the chickens had to scrounge for their pickings. The chickens' fare improved in fall, though, when Mom fed them grain gleaned from the spillage where the threshing machines had stood in neighbors' fields at harvest. Braving stickers, she scratched through the stubble with her bare hands to gather the spilled grain.

During this time another couple tried to convince my parents to move with them to California, where there was hope of work and relief from economic depression. My parents discussed the idea but then dismissed it, choosing instead to stay, to cast their lot on a family farm ... though it made no economic sense to do so.

I cannot speak for my father, but I know my mother never had regrets. At 78, long after my father's death, she wrote: "Today the wind is blowing, blowing in the memories of the winds, the heat, the drought of the Thirties. They were happy days—our early marriage. There seemed to be no sadness and no worries. We had each other and life was good. So! We lived on $4 a month and had no flour. No matter!"

Staying is what most farmers and ranchers do, when we can, when money permits. Indeed, you could say staying—waiting—is a long-ingrained habit among farmers, a trust. Everything about farming requires waiting, a conviction that tiny seeds planted in bare earth will come to life in the soil, a trust that lush green shoots growing from the seeds will yield a harvest of grain, and that this harvest will become food, either to stay on the farm or to be sold. Herds of cattle and flocks of sheep or chickens—these all take time to build. Indeed, it can take decades to develop herds of livestock with the genetics a farmer or rancher envisions. Each crop of calves requires a gestation period, a year of waiting. Farmers understand . . . no, they count on God's promise written in the Book of Isaiah:

"Before she was in labor she gave birth; before her pain came upon her she was delivered of a son. Who has heard of such a thing? Who has seen such things? Shall a land be born in one day? Shall a nation be brought forth in one moment? ... Shall I bring to the birth and not cause to bring forth? says the Lord; shall I, who cause to bring forth, shut the womb ... ."

And so John and I wait, expecting the gestation of our wait, of our work, to yield results, trusting even that results are coming that we may not be able to see for years, such as the slow return of plant vigor in overgrazed pastures, young trees growing voluntarily at slough edges, an increase of biological activity in the soil. We, like many other farmers and ranchers, have an economy of the heart that flies in the face of a monetary economy. Is it any wonder then that many farmers or ranchers are in the habit of staying, in the habit of waiting? We are compelled to stay, even when the economics look bleak; even after the last dollar is spent.

"This work comes from the heart," exclaims a North Dakota ranch partner, indignant about how farmers and ranchers are made to feel ashamed about conducting their lives more as a way of life than as a business. If this were not a way of life, she reasons, what else would cause ranchers to go out repeatedly during the long nights of spring, going without sleep to midwife cows and calves—in years when low prices steal profits? This from a woman who ran her own business in town for years to help the family ranch get on its feet.

An Iowa woman who owns and manages one of the state's top-producing dairy herds says to me during a telephone interview for an article: "I don't even really care about our production records. I just do the work because I like it. I love to see those little calves get out and run in the spring. When I get a heifer calf out of one of my best cows, I feel like it's Christmas again! Dairying is full of new promises."

We are a called people. I say this realizing that the word "called" means different things to different people. It is one of those words people often use generically. Most of us are not called as Moses was, by God's voice speaking from a burning bush. I wish it were so, for it seems it would be clear then, the direction in which one should walk, a question I often find perplexing. Most of us just do the best we can in judging what is our calling. We simply follow our hearts into the type of work we love. If life has shaped into a specific direction our heart-felt longings and the long-term events touching our lives, can we not presume, then, that this constitutes a measure of calling?

Where there is a calling, there is meaning. And where life has meaning, there is a deep, abiding resiliency to difficulty and uncertainty, even a good measure of peace of mind. Because of that, I feel rich.

A PRAYER FOR THE PRAIRIE

* * *

It is now early evening as I continue walking down the road, heading west of the farm. The sun is near setting, and it spills a soft, golden light across the snow-covered fields. I pass a frozen wetland where the fuzzy, dried heads of cattails look like thick cigars. The sun's low rays lend a backlight, silhouetting the cigar heads with an edging of gold. Straight ahead, barely a mile away, lies the hamlet of Kief. A tiny Baptist church sits at the edge of town. The church was built in 1901 by Ukrainian immigrants. It is the church where John and I spend some Sunday mornings. Inside at the front, is a plaque that once hung in our own house, before my parents moved there in 1946. The wall hanging belonged to the Linenko family, who homesteaded the farm in 1906. Before moving to California, the Linenkos donated the plaque to the little Baptist church, of which they were members. Written in a flowing Ukrainian hand, the words on the plaque quote the Apostle Paul briefly from the Book of First Corinthians: "You have been bought with a price."

I hear in these words a message about an economy of the heart, a mysterious economy of freedom. I am still learning the message of salvation inherent in these words. I am still learning their wide-sweeping inferences . . . about the value of human life, about the dignity of the human spirit. The words imply that we have been purchased through a mysterious but freeing exchange, an exchange transcending money and material conditions. We humans are of far too much value to be emotionally chained and shackled to debt, to endless earth-bound economic demands and expectations. Surely freedom from the anxiety and mechanistic behaviors and expectations imposed by these is our God-given heritage. Surely we should be free to let faith, hope, and love govern daily choices. I yearn for the strength and courage to accept this freedom.

I believe—oh, God, help my unbelief!—that as John and I move forward, deeper into this life forged in partnership with the land, we will find the shekels of a simple but profound prosperity.

As I walk down the road toward town, the setting sun lays a gilded swath of light across the hard snow, its surface etched by wind-swept ridges. The snow seems as white brocade laced with gold.

JOINING
FIELD TO FIELD
2001

May 25, 2001, was the last day the Stars and Stripes waved from the flagpole beside our small post office, an old false-fronted building on the Main Street of Kief. The U.S. Postal Service closed the post office, in effect, because it had too few patrons. The building was one of only two spheres of social life yet remaining in our tiny town of 13 people. Now there is but one: the small grocery store Bennie Krueger runs in a building added on to the old Standard gas station he has long since stopped operating.

The absence of the flag has stripped a bit of courage from us, robbed a share of our sense of worth. But perhaps even more painful than the loss of life for the post office, and the loss of the identity it bequeathed upon our community, was the loss of Rosie, the vibrant, sunny-natured postmaster who filled the old building with vitality. The warmth of her personality emanated outside, a beacon radiating out into the countryside, welcoming people to the post office. Driving to town to get the mail or to post letters had given folks living in the country an excuse to rub shoulders, to exchange civilities, to share small talk in a landscape where such chances grow slimmer by the year.

A handful of us threw a farewell party, and townsfolk as well as farmers turned out to bid Rosie and our post office goodbye. We crowded into the tiny front vestibule to give her gifts and cards, to share coffee and cookies, to commiserate with each other over our loss. With tears flowing, Rosie gave us each envelopes postmarked with the date the Kief post office died, a date marking the end of an era lasting some 90 years.

We are growing used to such closings. Maybe even growing numb. The Postal Service had threatened to close our post office before. But we protested with a petition and letters, and we won out. Yet it was merely a stay of execution. The circumstances of this final closing make us feel beset upon, conspired against.

"They've had it in for us since that last time they tried to close the post office; they were just biding their time," someone says. Yes, it's a conspiracy theory that lets us place blame on the outside. It gives us a tactile shape on which to target our hurt and sense of betrayal, our unspoken and indeed shapeless fears about what this bodes for the future of our community.

Still, we take this closing with some sense of resignation, acknowledging, I suppose, that the coming of this very day was inevitable. After all, we had already accepted another major closing— that of the Kief Farmers Elevator only two years before. Of course, the elevator had been the town's center of commerce and trade. Farmers from miles around hauled truckloads of wheat, barley, and oats to be unloaded and stored in the tall wooden structure. As long as the elevator had room, farmers could sell grain there any day of the business week. Freight trains carried the grain to markets far beyond the hamlet of Kief, to millers in Minneapolis or Chicago, or to shipping docks on the Great Lakes. Besides serving as an outlet for our products, the elevator was a place we could buy supplies such as feed, salt, and mineral for cattle and hogs.

The elevator, too, had been a social draw. Stopping there to check on the price of wheat and feed oats was only partly a business affair; it was also partly a social event. Larry, the manager, was outgoing and jocular. His greeting to me seldom varied. "What's John up to today?" he'd ask. I took care in answering since I didn't know how my answer might be interpreted in jest back to my husband the next time it was he rather than me stopping at the elevator to pick up supplies.

Nevertheless, Larry's brief drilling made me smile, drew me out of myself, added life to my day. In Larry's absence, there is no replacement. My realm of people has shriveled because of the closing of the elevator. I used to go to town to mail packages, and I would stop at the elevator if we needed something. Now, our buying habits have changed. It is usually John who travels the longer distances to get farm supplies.

These closings impact others' buying patterns, too. People who once came to town to visit the elevator and post office would then commonly stop at Bennie's store for groceries. Many of these people no longer have a reason to come to Kief, and so they do their shopping in some bigger town, at some bigger grocery store.

Indeed, the lure of bigness caused the very downfall of the elevator. As farms have grown in size, farmers' harvests have burgeoned. Eighty years ago farmers hauled grain to town in wagons pulled by horses, wagons holding 50 to 60 bushels of wheat. Thirty years ago, my family hauled grain to this elevator in a truck carrying some 220 bushels of grain. Today, farmers harvest grain from their fields in volumes warranting the use of 800- to 1,000-bushel trailers pulled by diesel trucks. Given such mobility, grain growers can haul grain long distances to larger markets situated along major rail lines served by 100-unit trains. Because of the savings in rail charges, these huge outlets can afford to pay farmers 5 to 10 cents a bushel more for grain than the price paid by the small country elevators. Much of the grain trade, then, bypasses the smaller outlets.

And so, the streets of Kief grow more silent by the year. It was not always so. According to the town's oral history, 300 people lived there in 1918. Indeed, a photo taken of Main Street on the Fourth of July in 1911 shows a throng of people in the street and lining the sidewalks.

Even many years later, when I was small, Kief still brimmed with life. My mother, like many other people, did her grocery shopping in town on Saturday nights. As we drove into Kief, the big outdoor movie screen near the railroad tracks held court over an audience of people and parked cars. The sidewalk outside the Kief General Store, better known as Sam's Store, bustled with shoppers. Inside, store owner Sam Karpenko rang up grocery items and sliced meat and cheese in his stolid, unhurried manner. He set the stacks of slices on broad swaths of white paper laid on the counter. Then he deftly wrapped the edges of the paper up around each stack and tied it all tight with string pulled from a roll hanging overhead.

"Sam," my mother would sometimes ask, "do you happen to have any herring?"

"Yah, shoor!" Then the slow-speaking man with the Russian brogue would step to the deep barrel at the end of the counter, lift a whole herring from the salt brine and wrap it in wax paper.

"Yah, shoor!"

The words never changed. Calm, reassuring words. They echo down through the years. I hear them still when I am in my 20s, standing at that same counter, asking about some grocery item my mother needs. I have just come from Bennie Krueger's Standard station, getting spark plugs for the tractor. My hands are tough and temporarily blackened from working with wrenches amid oily engine debris. Yet I am comfortable in my skin. As Sam surely seems in his. The relaxed, unlined features of his face suggest a man who does not quarrel with life. We are, in that time, people of place and purpose.

Sam's store burned in 1981, and Sam died five years later. He had been a store owner in Kief for 51 years. Grass and spruce trees grow now where his store stood. Not even the footings of the old building remain, leaving an open, park-like place of silence spilling over into the lot where people once gathered on Saturday nights in the lee of the outdoor theater screen.

People of place and purpose?

I think we have all changed now. It is harder to be such people these days. We are more uncertain. Questioning. Wondering: Why did all the people leave?

Indeed, the town has become silent because the countryside has grown silent. According to one history book, the township surrounding our farm had 179 inhabitants in 1900. Most were immigrants from the Ukraine. Today, only 42 people live in the township, an area six miles square. In 1920 15,544 people lived in our county; it's home to 6,000 today.

Along just one three-mile stretch of gravel road crossing our community are six abandoned farms. Indeed, empty farmyards pepper the hills wherever we drive. The people have long since left, leaving behind grey buildings, and sometimes soaring spruce trees or thick lilac hedges, testaments to the care people once took of these places where they built their lives. Fewer and fewer people live in a setting where farms and fields grow larger and larger by the year.

Some days the solitude is palpable. When John's two sisters— Eileen and Hilda, who live in a more populated setting—come for a visit, Eileen jokes that she feels the urge to get out of bed in the middle of the night and drive her car up and down the road in order to hear the sound of traffic going by. We laugh.

But in pensive moments, I wonder: When will the depopulation stop? How few people will eventually live here? When John and I are old, how many farms will yet remain? These uneasy questions sometimes make me think of the prophet Isaiah's words: "Woe to those who join house to house, who add field to field, until there is no more room, and you are made to dwell alone in the midst of the land. ... Surely many houses shall be desolate, large and beautiful houses, without inhabitant."

I can see that we are beginning "to dwell alone."

Have the people left because they were squeezed out as farms grew larger and larger? Or have the farms grown larger because the people decided to go away, leaving fewer and fewer people amongst whom to divide the land? Have poor crop prices been the culprit? Was it escalating costs? Was it the change from localized to more distant markets for farm products? Or have people simply left because they or their children thought they could find a better life in the city? Or, indeed, have all these things played a role?

Living as John and I do in the midst of the unsettling, surrounded daily by telltale signs of shrinking life, such questions are seldom far from my mind. Yet at the same time they are rhetorical. Even if the answers came marching into my dreams as clear as figurines, how would that change the fact of what already is? John and I can only look to our own farm, holding our questions as a context for the decisions we must make regarding our own situation. For indeed, we hope to stay. And yet we yearn to do much more than stay. We yearn to thrive as farmers, as full-time tenders of land and livestock, as caretakers of this place on earth.

That poses a central question: What size farm do we need in order to thrive? How large should our herd of cattle be, for instance?

These questions are simple on the surface only, and their answers are far from arbitrary, involving a delicate, complex matter of balance. We believe there is a simple law of sufficiency that can produce a life and work where pressures are in balance, where the potential for natural as well as financial crises are greatly diminished. There is a certain size, a balance, a mix of enterprises, a rhythm of work and life for us and for our farm that will make an efficient use of our energy, our skills, and aptitudes as we work with the soil, plants, and water comprising this farm. There is a rhythm of work and recreation, a mix of tasks, that will give us a sense of freedom, rather than a sense of bondage.

The possibility of tapping into such a mysterious law of sufficiency occurs to me when I read about God's dealings with the Israelites while they wandered for 40 years in the desert. The Book of Exodus says that while the Israelites wandered in the desert, they complained to Moses because they had no food. So God sent manna from heaven, instructing the people to gather an omer of manna per person each morning, except on the Sabbath. (An omer is a unit of measurement.) According to the biblical account: " ... they gathered, some more, some less. But when they measured it with an omer, he that gathered much had nothing over, and he that gathered little had no lack; each gathered according to what he could eat."

Some of the Israelites tried to hoard their manna, by not eating all their omer's worth each day. They were saving up, I suppose, thinking there might come a day when God would go back on His word and fail to send the daily provision of manna. But the hoarded manna quickly spoiled.

The exception was that double batch God instructed them to gather on the sixth day, so that they could have food on the Sabbath without having to go into the desert and gather on their day of rest. This extra manna, ordained as it was by God, did not spoil.

If it is indeed possible, as these passages imply, to live according to a law of simple sufficiency, striking a gentle balance between work and recreation, I wonder: How do John and I find that law, a law that will let our spirits and our bodies, our work and this farm endure and thrive?

Having posed the question, I find myself stumped for an answer. Rather, I should say, I can envision the answer, yet I do not know how to breathe life into the vision. Indeed, we believe a simple law of sufficiency lies at the core of our goals: to own no more cows than what we can provide feed for using mostly horses for power and low-cost haying equipment, and to operate on no more land than the family land to which we have a heritage—my parents' 468 acres and my grandparents' 700 acres of lakes and grassland.

But though I dislike the term, an economy of scale does indeed impact and seemingly challenges this simple process we envision. Given the average conventional market price for beef calves during the past decade, the calculator tells us we need at least 70 outstanding cows in order to earn the modest living we envision from this land. At an average income of some $450 per 550-pound calf, 70 cows would earn, at the absolute best—meaning no deaths and 100-percent conception—an annual income of $31,500.

We envision this amount to be nearly sufficient. Besides providing a family living, this sum would also cover operating costs such as gas for vehicles, machinery repairs, and supplies like seed and baler twine. It would also cover real estate taxes and a payment on the land. But $31,500 covers these expenses just barely. There would be no money left to service debt other than land debt and little left for vehicle and equipment replacement—even to replace small, horse-drawn equipment. We will probably continue to depend on my writing business for some years to provide a cushion for additional and unexpected expenses.

Still . . . the major question looms: How does one acquire the cows with which to earn the living, without depending so heavily on an off-the-farm income? If we borrow the money to buy them, a big chunk of our farm income must go toward servicing the debt, leaving us short on money to meet our other needs. The solution (and this is the typical philosophy farmers have taken in recent decades and certainly the one with which John and I were raised) might be to simply expand, to buy more and more cows until the income can cover all debt payments along with costs for operating and family living.

But, buying more cows would then require leasing more land for hay production, or buying more hay. It would also require buying the better haying equipment we would need in order to put up the larger amount of hay we could no longer put up by small equipment and labor-intensive means. That would mean additional debt on top of what we would have to borrow in order to buy the additional cows.

Like most farmers, John and I have lived with indebtedness for a long time. I would that we were like those who have planned well enough, or who have had the good fortune to come into agriculture without the need of borrowed capital. Too often, debt dictates circumstances. As a farm economist once told me in an interview: "Most decisions made at the kitchen table revolve around debt payments."

Life—especially life on a farm, impacted as it is by the unpredictabilities of weather and market prices—is too fluid to be bound by a structured chain of debt payments, which reduce the worth of farmers' and ranchers' work to a matter of financial performance. Wendell Berry writes in *The Unsettling of America*: "The concentration of farmland into larger and larger holdings and fewer and fewer hands— with the consequent increase of overhead, debt and dependence on machines—is thus a matter of complex significance, and its agricultural significance cannot be disentangled from its cultural significance. It forces a profound revolution in the farmer's mind: once his investment in land and machines is large enough, he must forsake the values of husbandry and assume those of finance and technology. Thenceforth his thinking is not determined by agricultural responsibility, but by financial accountability and the capacities of his machines. ... The economy of money has infiltrated and subverted the economies of nature, energy, and the human spirit."

John and I envision the greatest freeing of our spirits—and the most flexible and unfettered use of our land—to come in the years ahead, when we see the possibility of being debt free and eventually downsizing our herd to 40 or 50 cows. The beauty of the smaller-sized herd is that it would permit our hay-production system to rely more heavily on low-cost horse power and more manual labor. By lowering our costs still further, we would increase our profit margin.

We hope to widen the profit margin further—even with an eventual downsizing of the herd—by capturing more value from the beef we produce. We may try to market our weanling calves, raised solely on their dams' milk and forages, directly to consumers who would be willing to pay a premium over the supermarket price they pay for beef. The process would let us produce less volume of beef at less cost for a higher value at the farm gate. In sum, we hope to produce less for less expense, selling what we produce for a higher price. But our direct-marketing skills are untried; only time will tell how we fare.

* * *

There is no question that trends in the marketplace, causing low prices in relationship to those of decades past, have served to hamstring the profitability farmers and ranchers are able to earn from producing food. This spawns the tendency among us to continue expanding. It is a perplexing state, giving rise to a chicken-or-the-egg question: Have farmers as a culture embraced technology and labor-saving machinery at such a rate as to simply produce too much food, creating an excess that the marketplace has gotten into a complacent habit of undervaluing? Or have the lower prices resulted first from concentration among processing and marketing companies and their lavish use of costly processing, packaging, and advertising—which causes them to try to purchase raw products from farmers as cheaply as possible?

Now, these processes and this imbalance in what consumers pay for groceries and what farmers receive for their food products is entrenched in our culture. Given general buying patterns, there seems no other conclusion to be drawn than that mainstream consumers now expect to be wooed and pampered with processing, packaging, and convenience by the corporations supplying products for edible consumption—products barely resembling the natural food from which they originated.

Whatever the cause, the result is a chokehold on price at the farm gate and relatively cheap food for consumers. According to a 1997 report prepared by Integrity Systems Cooperative for the United States Department of Agriculture's Sustainable Agriculture Research and Education Program, what Americans pay for food amounts to about 12 percent of their disposable income—the smallest percentage of income paid for food of any high-income country. Still, from 1975 to 1993, the report continues, the retail price of food increased by 18 percent—in excess of inflation.

Yet, the farmer's share of the food dollar has dwindled to a pittance, earning us little more than 4 percent of its value, according to information compiled in 1999 by Dr. Curtis Stofferahn, a University of North Dakota rural sociologist.

Furthermore, the distribution and marketing systems of our present, globalized food-distribution system are becoming increasingly concentrated in the hands of just a few transnational firms. Stofferahn says that the four largest firms control the processing of about 80 percent of beef cattle, 57 percent of hogs and 50 percent of broilers produced in the United States. These four largest firms also purchase 57 to 76 percent of the corn, wheat, and soybeans grown in this country.

In the paper "Feeding the Village First," produced for the Northern Plains Sustainable Agriculture Society, North Dakota organic farmer Fred Kirschenmann, who also directs the Leopold Center for Sustainable Agriculture in Iowa, writes: "The globalization and industrialization of agriculture has reduced farmers in North Dakota to raw-materials suppliers of a few specialized commodities—primarily wheat and beef cattle. ... That, in turn, means that we export all of our cheap raw materials and import all of our needed, expensive value-added products. This drains both the wealth of the region's income and the wealth potential of the region's raw materials out of our local communities."

This fact became glaringly evident to me one morning two summers ago. I had just finished milking my three dairy cows by hand and was lingering in the barn, considering the pails of milk before setting aside our house milk and giving the rest to the dairy calves we were feeding that summer. Having grown up as I had, always viewing milk as a commodity, I couldn't help but wonder how valuable the milk was that I had in my buckets, if I were to sell it. Back in the house, I figured it out: Since two of the cows were nearing the end of their lactations, the total from the three cows for two milkings a day came to 88 pounds, or 11 gallons. Sold at a bulk milk price (that is, raw to the processor) of 12 cents per pound, the milk would have earned $10.56. But the cost of the grain to feed the cows amounted to about $6.50 a day, leaving a profit margin of $4.06 for the 11 gallons from the three cows.

Yet the price we paid [in 2000] for milk at the grocery store amounted to $3.78 per gallon. Though governmental health regulations keep me from selling my milk by conventional means directly to consumers, were I indeed to receive the store price for the milk in my buckets, the sum I would have earned from the 11 gallons my cows gave amounted to $41.58 a day, or about $35 after grain costs, for just an hour's worth of mostly pleasant work twice a day, work that includes walking the cows up from the pasture.

If consumers shared in the delivery costs, this simple, brief task of hand-milking my cows has the potential to earn $1,050 per month—that is, if I were not hampered by regulations and were free to sell milk to customers who had visited our farm and who endorsed my hand-milking methods and the management of our cows. For this small number of cows (six, assuming I wanted to earn the income from them year-round, milking three for half a year at a time), it would be easy to put up enough winter forage for the cows by low-cost, horse- and human-powered methods.

Since the price of the bulk milk is so low relative to feed costs and other costs associated with the larger number of cows needed to earn a livelihood from the slim profit margin, dairies, of course, are getting larger and larger. Many dairies now milk thousands of cows. For that reason, small dairy operations have been nearly wiped out in North Dakota. Now, in 2001, some farmers who once depended on dairying work in town at full-time jobs paying $6 to $9 an hour, or $1,000 to $1,500 a month.

* * *

Though consumers' interests are shifting in ways that are opening ground in which more sustainable, localized food systems might take root, obstacles remain. One is the price consumers are willing to pay for products produced through the use of less industrialized, more sustainable practices. The current price of supermarket food—which is produced by globalized, industrialized methods—seems to serve as the yardstick consumers use when comparing food prices. However, when food is produced and marketed in small volumes or produced by alternative means that are often more labor intensive, it's difficult in many instances for farmers to earn a profit from food sales when the supermarket price serves as the upper limit consumers are willing to pay.

"If [supermarket] food were priced at its true cost, however," says Stofferahn, "the price would be much higher than it is now. The externalities—the environmental destruction and the human illnesses caused by the industrialized, globalized food system—are not figured into our present food costs."

According to Stofferahn's research from 1999, these are a few of the external costs present food prices fail to reflect:

* The food system accounts for 16 percent of the energy consumed in the United States. Processing, packaging, transportation, and marketing account for 75 to 85 percent of this energy use.

* Packaging costs exceed the value of the food itself; 33 percent of solid wastes in landfills are packaging wastes.

* Soil erosion occurs at a rate of 7 tons per acre per year, or 14 times the rate of replenishment in this country. The cost of this soil erosion amounts to about $44 billion per year.

More localized systems of food production and distribution, of course, once shaped the framework on which family farms were built. Local grocers bought eggs from farmers' small flocks, for instance. Some towns had creameries where farmers sold milk and cream. The creameries, in turn, supplied neighboring towns with dairy products. Local flour mills and butcher shops bought grain and meat animals from farmers and resold these as processed products such as flours, cereals, and sausage.

John and I are only one generation removed from this tradition. I remember, for instance, cleaning eggs for my mother to pack in layers in a big wooden crate. She would take these eggs to Kief and sell them to store owner Sam Karpenko. Before expanding the dairy herd, we sold cream. Mom hauled this to Kief, too, in five-gallon cans. The small creamery stood on Main Street, just north of Sam's store.

My parents thrived under this more localized farming economy. They rented their first farm of 160 acres in 1936. Even though their meager start began in the sunset years of the Great Depression, still, they were able to buy that farm, sell it, and pay cash for a larger farm just 10 years later, in 1946. Soon, by renting additional land, my father, who did not believe in borrowing money, soon grew grain on some 900 acres and owned a string of new equipment. But the expansion did not guarantee sustained prosperity. A year of drought followed a year when the crops were hailed out. The reduced income forced my mother back to teaching the year I turned six. As fall melded into winter, my father said to her, partly in jest, "You better teach a little faster."

March brought my father's death, and of course, the economics of the farm changed.

In time, Mom let go of the rented land, and borrowed money to buy 68 acres of new land. She also upgraded buildings, bought more cattle, and expanded the dairy. But with changing markets and escalating farm costs, she was not able to maintain the cash-basis system of operating under which she and Dad had farmed together. She was forced to enter a cycle of debt to accomplish the expansion, which indeed proved profitable for a number of years.

But by the time John and I returned to the farm in 1990, Mom's expansion was long out-dated. We would have had to expand either the land base or the dairy again in order to draw a livelihood from either dairying or grain farming managed according to a conventional production system. This would have required a new cycle of debt added on top of the fragments of the old cycle still remaining from my mother's expansion.

"When do we get off the merry-go-round of debt?" John asks.

Indeed . . . when?

When will we, along with so many other farmers and ranchers, discover freedom from the deadlines of heavy and constraining debt payments? When will the cream of our energies, the best of our years, the most fertile ground of our creativity and imagination stop being eroded down the drainhole of a repayment schedule for excessive debt?

Maybe it's simpler than we think to continue farming without being burdened by excess cost and huge debt loads, in spite of the fact that, aside from income earned from direct marketing to consumers, market prices are largely beyond our control. Maybe it is, indeed, only a matter of careful planning and, then, simply stepping off the merry-go-round.

Maybe this freedom can only begin first in our own minds. Maybe it begins from a simple willingness to confront fearlessly and objectively the paradigms—the assumed regulations—upon which we have built our lives. Maybe these paradigms are no more than rusted, worn-out cages, with doors ajar—and we have not yet even noticed that we are free to step from within their confines at the moment of our choosing.

But, indeed, paradigms are comfortable; they represent convention, conformity, familiarity. The terms of their confinement are "known." By contrast, seeking freedom from these poses risk . . . and the prospects of entering an uncharted wilderness.

* * *

I hope John and I have the courage to continue testing the gates of our perceived boundaries; I hope we will grow the will and insights we need to take to the wilderness as we seek new ways to prosper while tending this land. I pray that we have the courage to gather only that which is sufficient, accepting the freedom hidden in an omer's worth of manna.

THE LAND PROVIDES

2002

Overhead, a strong wind rushes through the bare tops of the cottonwoods with a sound akin to the roar of a river cascading down a dangerous rapids. I stand at the gate to a pen of heifers, waiting, ready to open it for John and his team of horses, Pete and Skeet, when they come from the field with a bale of hay for the young cattle.

They should have come by now, I worry. Out in the open, just beyond the boundary of the cottonwood trees east of the pen, the wind drives the snow in a grey wall before it. Peering toward the field, I can see nothing but murky white. Is it possible, I wonder, that John and the horses have lost their sense of direction in the swirling snow? Or maybe the wind has spooked Pete and Skeet, and they have run away with John and the sled?

My experience with blizzards past will linger forever in the fringes of my memory. Those who have seen them at their worst may be forever wary, always cautious, respectful of Mother Nature's power . . . and whims.

There are old legends, too, that are made more vivid and alive by my own experiences with choking, blinding blizzards. The most vivid of these yarns is the legend of Hazel Miner: Hazel's ordeal happened in 1920. With her younger brother and sister, she attended a one-room school on the wide-open prairie a couple of miles from her farm home. One fateful day, as morning gave ground to afternoon, the sky turned from benign to belligerent. Dark, angry clouds boiled up from the west.

Soon a northerly wind bellowed around the corners of the schoolhouse, and a white, blinding wall of heavy snow smothered the view through the windows. Hazel's father came from home to help his children drive their horse and sleigh home. But father and children became separated in the blinding, driving snow. The children and their faithful horse got lost, and the sleigh overturned. Hazel gave her life to the blizzard that day, sheltering her siblings from the snow and wind with her own body that they might live.

And so, because I have been reared on such legends and because I have had my own brushes with treacherous blizzards, I do not underestimate the power of the wind and the snow as I peer intently toward the east, hoping that the dim outline of my husband driving his team will soon emerge from the swirling murk. In time, they come, and a great weight lifts; a sense of suspended reality passes. The heifers, just weaned from their mothers, are ravenous over the hay, jerking big mouthfuls from the bale, more in frustration than hunger. Oblivious, of course, to my few anxious moments, they have been fretting themselves, walking about the pen bellowing for their mothers. Their pain of loss will pass in a couple of days, and they will soon settle down to a calm routine of eating, drinking, and sleeping.

The hay the heifers wolf down is the product, of course, from a kinder day than this, a summer season of warmth and rain when the land basks in its own beauty, a beauty that begins and matures slowly as the harsh hand of winter lifts gradually with the coming of spring and slips skulking into the north as summer blooms. Surrounded as we are in the moment by a stark blanket of white covering the ground and the naked limbs of trees pointing like gnarled fingers at indiscernable objects, it seems such a beauty could never be.

Yet the green meadow hay the heifers eat is a testament: Winter indeed passes, and the land provides. Some years more so than others, and some years, when drought comes, to a small degree. Yet, always something. Unfailing. Unwavering. No matter how many angry days of winter come, the pain and discomfort of this frozen season eventually dissolve into the soft days of spring, and the snow soon gives way to green plants. I know this with my mind and memory. But with the tentative, foreboding feeling fostered by the blizzard still tugging at my gut, I yearn for a sense of spring. Later in the evening, back in the house, I dig out my journal and read an entry from the middle of June. It is an account of an ethereal Sunday when I "walked in God's cathedral." The day began when I was awakened by bird songs:

"It was hot last night," I wrote. "It was the birds, I think, that woke me. The Western kingbirds start singing about four a.m., when just a hint of morning light begins to lift the darkness. The kingbirds sing in rounds, their song washing over the dusk in waves. The robins chime in a bit later, and the mourning doves soon after.

"By about five, other sounds caught my hear: Cows bellowing and a bull growling loudly from the northeast, from the direction where one herd of cows and calves are pasturing. I considered getting out of bed to check on the cattle, but a thick fog cloaked the morning with an impenetrable veil of grey. By the time the fog began to give way to full-blown light, John, awakened too by the ruckus, headed to the pasture in the pickup. I came on foot, walking on the trail north of the yard. The scene and sounds caused me to stop at the knoll just southeast of the dugout where the cows come to water: The remaining fog covered the fields with a quilt of translucent white. The clear sky above the fog was grey-blue, and a dim half-moon hung in the sky. Dew clothed the pasture, causing the feathered heads of the mature June grass to appear drenched in hoar frost.

"The bird songs comprise a virtual orchestra," my journal continued. "From every quarter a meadowlark sings. Nearby, a red-winged blackbird perches atop a fence post, caroling. From farther afield, a host of red-winged and yellow-headed blackbirds trill and chortle from the sloughs where they perch amid the reeds. From a greater distance comes the song of an upland sandpiper. The sandpiper's melody begins with a sensuous trill and shifts into a drawn-out call not unlike the sound of a lazy wolf whistle."

I recall from that day that as I stood on the knoll, watching, listening, basking in the music and in the colors and textures of the scene, I was enveloped by a familiar sense of oneness with this place, a sense that if I could shed my body, my spirit would simply pass like vapor into the elements of this Artist's canvas.

Such memories of summer sustain hope in winter. Indeed, they are reminders that a season of bitter cold holds purpose. Because from these contrasting worlds—the stiff, cold hands of winter and the nimble bare feet of summer—life is born on the northern plains. A season of death and decay dissolves into renewed life. Burgeoning life, life bursting at the seams. It begins before the snow melts. It starts when the birds belonging to warmer seasons return. They are the harbingers of spring, and they come back long before the leafing of the trees and the greening of the grass.

Longing to hear songs other than those of the wintering birds, such as the sparrows, starlings, and chickadees, I begin to question John in January: "When will the summer birds be back?" He turns to his calendar and reads what he has recorded last spring: "The first eagles were back Feb. 5; we saw the first crows on March 2; geese on March 17; blackbirds on March 19, and meadowlarks on April 2."

As the snow melts into the earth, sprigs of green poke up through the carpet of plant duff, brown leavings from last fall. The cool-season grasses and forbs, like thin-stemmed crested wheatgrass and the sprawling tendrils of dandelions, are among the first plants to come to life. As the sun's warmth lingers longer and longer each day, more plants awaken from winter's slumber, and soon the fields, ravines, and meadows are blanketed in glistening greenery and reverberate with bird and insect sounds.

But the circle of life on this farm is not without what we—or I— perceive to be flaws. Sometimes it seems to proceed from day to day, season to season, with an obstinate bent, determined to thwart at all costs the efforts of humans to turn its course. Yet, when John and I stand still and consider this cycle of life in its entirety, its humble progress seems thunderous.

Still, not everyone sees what we see. Not long ago John came home from town, recounting an exchange he had had with a farmer from some miles away. The man asked John where we farmed. Learning the spot, he said: "Oh, I've been by that place. Nothing happens there!"

John replied, "Well, two people happen to make their full-time living on that farm."

I am mindful of this man's comment the next time I go for a walk down the main road. Questioningly, I look back at our farm, trying to see the nothingness that the farmer saw. Try as I might, I cannot. What I see instead is a living, dynamic tapestry of grass, wetlands, cottonwood trees, and willow bushes growing voluntarily at slough edges; fields of alfalfa, patches of weeds, round bales of hay in one field, stacks of loose hay in a field beyond; horses grazing south of the yard; sheep lambing in June under the bushy canopy of a wormwood patch, and cows grazing pasture paddocks in fields where quack grass predominates. It is a tapestry that may seem wild, messy, unpatterned to most. Indeed, sometimes it seems so even to me. Maybe this seeming messiness, this lack of a conventional pattern, is what the farmer meant: "Nothing happens there!"

Yet this farm has a life of its own, free, unfettered. It evolves; its very character changes, not just from season to season, but from year to year. I struggle to let go of my structured expectations of life and farming conditions; I must consciously work at emotionally granting the land the freedom to express its own character; I must consciously work at adjusting my emotional reactions to what the land decrees, rather than forcing my expectations on the land.

Farming—as John and I have known it most of our lives—is, largely, a culture of control; a culture of humans trying to control nature. But we are striving now to break free from mongering control over nature. We are, instead, trying to learn to farm in hands-off ways that respond to, rather than control, nature's rhythms. These are hard, often painful lessons for me to learn. They come much easier for my husband, who is more patient and intuitive in his responses to the earth's cycles and its processes.

But we have learned enough so far to see that putting more control back in the hands of nature results in increased biodiversity. This is my husband's intent, and in our discussions about our interactions with the land, he describes his thoughts: "If you encourage biodiversity so that it occurs in amounts large enough, it surrounds everything you touch, and it's an ongoing process. By some standards it would be called messy farming. Yet it's a creation that is there by intent. It certainly doesn't happen accidentally. Because of this biodiversity the land does provide, yet it's much more than a nutritional provision that can be measured in bushels of grain or tons of hay per acre. Through biodiversity nature provides the healing balances it needs in order to remain healthy."

Trying to understand, indeed, simply fathom, what "healing balances" might be at work in the simplest processes of this farm—say, a cow nonchalantly grazing flower heads from the tops of Canada thistle plants when she is otherwise surrounded by lush grass—requires a studious, reflective consideration of a host of natural variables. To name a few: the immediate nutritional demands of the cow, the growth stage of the thistles; weather, moisture, and soil conditions.

Trying to perceive the healing balances becomes almost a spiritual, intuitive process of piecing together a puzzle for which you do not know the image beforehand. The impetus for studying the connections is our conviction that a strong current of synergy underlies the interactions between insects, birds and soils, for instance; and between soils and plants, between plants and animals on this farm; and between humans with the whole of this life. John and I trust that learning to live and work in harmony with this synergy, working out patterns of farming whose rhythms are rooted in it, will produce a holistic impact that will have a greater consequence than the economic sum total of the individual parts of the whole.

But we are merely learners of such thinking. It is an ongoing lesson in humility to relearn, year in and year out, that God decrees a rhythm for the land each year in accordance with a broader scheme that seems, at times, too vast to grasp. This scheme, outside our realm of understanding, keeps us looking, waiting, seeking to understand, searching for ways to respond to the land that are appropriate for each new condition.

I am reminded of our need for humility and watchfulness when I read these words from the Book of Ezekiel: "Thus says the Lord God: 'I myself will take a sprig from the lofty top of the cedar, and will set it out; I will break off from the topmost of its young twigs a tender one, and I myself will plant it upon a high and lofty mountain; on the mountain height of Israel will I plant it, that it may bring forth boughs and bear fruit, and become a noble cedar; and under it will dwell all kinds of beasts; in the shade of its branches birds of every sort will nest. And all the trees of the field shall know that I the Lord bring low the high tree, and make high the low tree, dry up the green tree, and make the dry tree flourish. I the Lord have spoken, and I will do it.'"

We have not come gently to this acknowledgment that God is the Gardener, and not we ourselves. It has dawned upon us gradually, after a long season of struggle and strife, a season of ignoring our own aptitudes, a season of trying to wrest forcefully from this land what it did not yet want to yield.

When we took over the management of my mother's farm in 1990, circumstances soon caught us up in what we perceived to be a demanding web of economic necessity. We needed to generate income not only for ourselves, but also for my mother, in the form of land rent. We also needed to earn money to repay bank notes for money borrowed to buy used farm machinery as well as to pay for annual operating expenses, such as seed, tractor fuel, and repairs.

Though we had come to the farm with the intention of only raising cattle, mounting economic needs soon prompted us to consider growing grain to sell also. That increased the amount of equipment we needed to buy. And because the fields had long since reverted naturally to quack grass, a grass many farmers consider to be a serious weed, we incurred a fair bit of expense getting the fields in shape to raise grain. In lieu of using herbicides we cultivated the fields numerous times in order to break up the sod and subdue the stubborn quack grass. But the more we tilled the fields, the harder Mother Nature worked to re-cover the soil with weeds as well as with quack grass.

Another problem was that natural soil fertility, too, seemed lacking, causing reduced yields in some fields. Fertility can be improved naturally with applications of animal manure and "green manure" from legume crops that are tilled back into the earth. But this process of restoring natural fertility and suppressing weeds through a natural but complex scheme of crop rotation can take several years before it results in improved yields.

Yet even my use of the phrase "improved yields" leads to a more basic question: How much is enough? For decades now, the status quo for crop yields is set by the average yields in a county, for instance, from fields where chemical fertilizers are used to inject fertility, and where chemical herbicides and pesticides are used in place of crop rotation to achieve weed and insect control. As a commercial agricultural journalist, I, too, have used the phrase "conventional average yield" as a yardstick against which to attempt to measure the success of organic agriculture as it is practiced by those farmers who have worked out crop-rotation sequences and tillage practices that indeed result in crop yields that measure up, so to speak, to "the conventional average yield" of the area.

So, stuck in the conventional mindset, we took a farm plan each spring to our lender that listed a target amount for yields of crops that, in retrospect, was unrealistic for the natural processes of this farm. Each spring we borrowed money against this target. But our yields—and our ability to repay the loan—often fell short, requiring annual refinancing of the economic shortfall, in addition to a new year's operating loan. Some other farmers also experience this recycling of debt. How could it be otherwise, when you consider this information from the paper "Feeding the Village First," authored in the late 1990s by North Dakota organic farmer Fred Kirschenmann, who also directs Iowa's Leopold Center for Sustainable Agriculture:

" ... it now costs North Dakota farmers $117 an acre to produce wheat. Most county-wide average wheat yields in North Dakota run below 30 bushels an acre. That means farmers need to consistently get at least $4 per bushel just to break even on their input costs. But given global-wide surplus production in 1998, prices hovered at $2.50 per bushel. So farmers find it impossible to generate the cash to repay loans or purchase inputs for the next crop cycle." That is why many farmers rely on farm-program payments to help make up the economic shortfall.

For John and me, the process of trying to control Mother Nature by overwhelming her with a mechanical advantage very nearly broke us. In the end, economics forced us to sell even the few cattle we owned. Without the livestock and the manure the animals contribute to the soil, we were stripped further of our ability to restore natural fertility to the land. We were stuck in a vicious circle of high costs and low income.

But in the eighth and ninth years of our farming experience, we finally "stopped the madness," as it is my habit to describe how events transpired. In comparison to the striving of previous years, we stood still, so to speak, doing only the field operations for which we could pay cash. It was not by choice. We simply had no more breathing space left in our ability to borrow operating money from the bank. We owned no cattle, except for the four cows given to us by my brother John and his wife, Mary. With only four cows for whom to put up winter feed, John sold most of the hay we grew on fields previously planted to grain. We were able to raise the hay cheaply because planting oats and peas mixed and harvesting the crop for feed is a cheaper process than carefully preparing fields for grain and then swathing the crop down, and harvesting the grain from the swaths with a combine. Our operating money came mostly from my sales of magazine articles. It was a time of walking in the dark in slow motion, continually bumping into seemingly blind alleys.

At the same time, my aging mother, whose home we now shared, required increasing care. Overriding our financial paralysis was our determination to try to provide the sort of care for my mother that would give her the freedom to continue living in her own setting, amid her beloved rural surroundings, rather than in a nursing home.

With my hope and once-exuberant energy long spent, I observed with a sort of detached fascination that as my mother's needs for personal care increased, her expectations of income from the farm decreased. Indeed, my aging mother's truest needs seemed to be met in ways increasing in abundance in what appeared to be a direct proportion to the degree to which she dropped her financial expectations of us as we groped our way through a dark valley.

Our days passed in what seemed like slow motion: Even through the summer I worked long days at the computer, writing articles for agricultural publications. I served meals and medications to my mother, managed her clothing and helped her with bathing. In the afternoons, before having lunch with John, I had coffee with Mom. In warm weather we sat out on the east porch. Usually it was my mother who spoke, as we drank our rich, open-kettle-brewed coffee from big cups. She told stories from earlier days, or recounted the escapades of the swallows nesting at the upper edging of the porch. When weather permitted, Mom spent most of her time sitting outside, watching her swallows, and the mourning doves nesting in the spruce trees nearby.

Just northeast of the house John designed a flower bed from the forked log of an old cottonwood tree that had died. At the west end of the log he placed the wooden wheel from a derelict wagon that had served Dad and Mom in their early years of farming. At the east end of the log

John placed large field stones and the spoked hub from another of the old wagon's wheels. We planted flowers in the bed and kept the yard mowed and tended behind the house. Though we, too, of course, were blessed by the beauty that resulted, much of our effort was intended to enhance the beauty of my mother's surroundings, to add visual richness to her days, days growing increasingly stripped of sensory beauty as her hearing and mobility diminished.

The vegetables I served my mother we harvested from our own garden, and she ate whole-grain breads from my baking. Right up to eight weeks before my mother's death at the age of 89, the symptoms of her congestive heart failure seemed to go into a sort of remission, and her arthritis stabilized, permitting her to go for short walks to visit the flower bed and the fruit trees we had helped her plant and water several years before. Indeed, my mother seemed to experience a renewed capacity to feel joyful. Or maybe she experienced simply a renewed commitment to express joy. I cannot tell which. Maybe these processes are one and the same.

Yet, as my mother's joy seemed to grow, my own hope froze. I glimpsed my husband at work sometimes from the window, and I yearned to join him. Sometimes I did indeed shrug off my obligation to work at the computer and looked instead for outdoor tasks I could do.

Yet often, as John and I worked together, we were silent. Our talk of the future stilled. Sometimes I would notice, for instance, that field hay waited to be baled, yet the tractor and baler sat still in the yard. Our silence was too thick for discussion. I could only mentally sift through fragments of conversation from days past to recall that John had mentioned a breakdown. I could only assume, then, that the last payment I had received for an article had been used up, and there was no money left to purchase repairs. Thus, the farming operations were awaiting a new influx of cash from my computer. I assumed John did not want to pressure me by telling me this. He would simply wait until the money came.

This insight drove me back to the computer and the next article on my list.

Often, in the evenings I would walk to the top of the Big Hill east of the farmyard. I came to regard the hill as my Prayer Hill. But for as many days as my prayers took shape, there were more days that they were formless, comprising wordless times of staring down at the farmstead and the fields surrounding it. I often wondered, how had all this happened? How had we become stripped so naked of our dreams, so naked of our means of achieving them? How had we become so weakened in power, as the world defines power? Like the Israelites wandering in the wilderness and protesting against God, I demanded: "Why have You led us here only to permit our means of tending this place to be stripped away?"

The events bringing us to the farm in 1990 had converged together and propelled us forward as though we had been caught up in a rushing current permitting no turning back. It had seemed all part of a providential plan. Now I could not even "see" in my mind's eye the vision we once had, a vision of a farm filled with fertile fields and animal life, a life from which we could draw a livelihood. Conjuring the vision seemed a cruel form of emotional self-torment, drawing a taunt from some dark corner of my mind, saying it could never be.

Yet one day words from the prophet Isaiah snagged my imagination:

"I work and who can hinder it? ... Remember not the former things, nor consider the things of old. Behold, I am doing a new thing; now it springs forth, do you not perceive it? I will make a way in the wilderness and rivers in the desert."

I wrote the words on a card and placed the card beside my computer.

But if the words indeed sparked hope, it was too small to feel. With that by now familiar, detached fascination I simply wondered: Could it actually be that God is using this difficult time to create something new on this farm, something new from our lives and from our work?

The question fueled a dogged sort of perseverance, born more from curiosity than from hope. It was a sort of determination to see just what this new "thing" might be. Besides, we had little left to lose by persevering.

Still, as time passed, a sprig of hope took root again as our economic condition responded to the restraint we placed on our farming activities. Because we did not have so many fields to plant and harvest, and because we were running tractors and other machinery less and less, John and I noticed that our money did not slip away quite so quickly.

One day in early 1999 the insight came that we could build a cow herd calf by calf, that trying to start a herd again from meager beginnings might actually lead to the soundest financial outcome in the long run. And so we determined to buy, when our cash flow permitted, newborn heifer calves, one by one, from neighboring dairy farmers.

It was in late spring that John brought the first heifer home in a large wooden crate in the back of the pickup. When I heard him drive into the yard, I rushed outside to meet our new baby cow. She was black with a brownish tinge, deep-sided, with big innocent eyes. Her sleek hide glistened in the sun. She seemed a gift of a magnitude far exceeding her simple economic worth of just $120. We christened her Mustard, mindful of the mystery of Jesus' words: "With what can we compare the kingdom of God, or what parable shall we use for it? It is like a grain of mustard seed, which, when sown upon the ground, is the smallest of all the seeds on earth; yet when it is sown it grows up and becomes the greatest of all shrubs, and puts forth large branches, so that the birds of the air can make nests in its shade."

More Mustard Seed Heifers came to our farm that summer. And the next. In 2000 we bought a handful of Milking Shorthorn cows, one by one. That summer local ranchers brought us a small herd of cows to custom graze. The following summer came more cows from the same ranchers' herd, and we cared for these on shares, sharing the income from the calves with the owners. We kept three heifers from those cows.

And the oldest Mustard Seed Heifers had heifers. The herd mushrooms almost of its own volition.

Meanwhile, a mysterious process is at work in the fields as well: As we have lessened our grip of control on nature, the land provides in ways that are at once simple and yet complex. These provisions are spun from an interconnected web, hiding like the secret images of a clever artist's painting hide amid an intricate creation of shapes. And we are only beginning to discern these provisions, for we are learning that discernment requires a practiced eye.

An impetus for this process has been John's abandonment of old boundaries of fields. Not to make fields larger, but to make them smaller. When we took over the farm, the field boundaries were the same as they were during the days my father farmed the land. The farm's fields were originally laid out in an orderly arrangement: Ignoring natural variances in terrain, nearly all of the fields were arranged in neat rectangles, running from west to east. But John divided the fields further, in accordance to terrain, rather than a surveyor's eye for straight lines. Following the zigzag of the lowlands, he fenced these and converted them to small pastures. Some fields on higher land he seeded to alfalfa.

In still other fields we have simply continued "to stop the madness," stepping back from forcing land to be farmed that does not want to be farmed. In such fields we have neither tilled nor seeded, but only grazed cattle now and then, waiting, letting Mother Nature garden as she will. Today the Eighty, for instance, hardly resembles the wide-open place I recall from my youth.

One of my most vivid memories—which serves to illustrate the previous monoculture character of the field—comes from an early weekend evening when I was home from college. It was late fall, and the dairy cows were grazing the stubble at the far end of the field, which had been planted to grain that summer, grain that was now harvested. I set off on my Arabian stallion Deene to bring the cows home for the evening milking. The wind drove a cool, wet drizzle before it, fueling Deene's high spirits. With my bay horse just barely able to keep himself from bucking and with me singing at the top of my lungs a rock song celebrating life, we raced flat out across the Eighty on our way to the cows.

Today such a race would run into several obstacles. John has divided the 80-acre field into six parcels. Two grow hay crops, and four are paddocks fenced for grazing cattle. One of these paddocks extends into a neighboring field, which contains an alkaline lowland. The gumbo in this low spot, which was previously farmed for as long as I can remember, was treacherous to tractors when it was wet. And it stubbornly refused to grow anything but the scantiest of grain crops. Yet to cows this seemingly cantankerous corner of land is gentle, freely offering as food its covering of a medley of weeds, quack grass, and volunteer sweet clover. Each year its covering grows denser voluntarily. And we no longer quarrel with it.

Another of the grazing paddocks on the old Eighty has become one of our most productive pastures. It is a spot where quack grass thrives. The more often the cows graze this hardy grass and the more manure they leave behind to fertilize the field, the more the quack grass grows, despite relatively dry weather. In another of the grazing paddocks on the Eighty, several elm trees have sprung up voluntarily. John has fenced around these young trees, so that the cattle cannot rub on their limbs and graze their leaves. At the east edge of the old field, several cottonwoods and willows have sprung up. John has fenced these away from the cattle also. Partway down the field, a two-row shelterbelt of young caragana and green ash trees that we planted disects the field from north to south, extending straight across a neighboring 40-acre field.

The diversity of plants and natural borders in the field creates a diversity of "edge," as John explains it to me. In these numerous and diverse field edges, a variety of plants complete their life cycle, attracting a range of insects, of which 90 percent are beneficial to crops, according to ecologist Allan Savory. With the insects come their natural checks and balances—the birds. In sum, a mosaic of biodiversity is fostered, on the soil's surface as well as beneath it. In his book *Holistic Management* Allan Savory writes: "One of the quickest ways to increase the diversity of species in any environment, whether you are managing a garden, a ranch or farm, a stream or ocean inlet, is to increase the amount of *edge*—where two or more habitats join."

As our land evolves, assuming a more natural, freer character, John and I, too, feel freer, more patient, more trusting of the earth's natural processes, more trusting of the land's willingness to provide. Indeed, we experience a heightened sense of curiosity: What sort of life will evolve from the land in the years to come?

The words from Isaiah do indeed seem to hold a promise: "Behold, I am doing a new thing; now it springs forth, do you not perceive it?"

We wait and watch . . . and wonder: What plants will spring from the ground this year along with the young alfalfa plants "seeded" in a field by the cows' hooves lightly churning the soil? What plants will grow up amid and compete with the patches of Canada thistle growing in some of the paddocks the cows grazed last summer? How will the nature of our soil and plant life evolve as we use horses more and more for planting small plots of crops and for harvesting hay? Will the health of our cow herd continue to improve as their diet becomes even more diverse? How will the health of our own diet improve as we incorporate to an increasing degree those wild plants many call weeds, plants such as dandelions, sow thistle, and lamb's-quarters? What characteristics will this year's garden display, planted on land where John fed hay to the cows the winter before last? Will the health of our own bodies remain stable and possibly even improve, despite aging, so that we can continue to work alongside our cattle and horses in the tending of this place and the harvesting of its food?

Indeed, I believe I do see the blurred edges of a new image taking shape from the Artist's canvas that is this farm. From the fragments of the image that are discernable to my eye, I perceive a deep mystery: that John and I are present on this land to the same degree that its myriad of insects and soil microogranisms are present; we are present to the same degree that the birds and the diverse plants of the fields and sloughs are present. This process of a shared dependency among levels of life, a process we now perceive at work on our own farm, we heard ecologist Allan Savory discuss in a lecture more than a decade ago.

Savory said, in sum: The loss of biological diversity begins with the loss of some insects, some birds, some butterflies. As the biological diversity continues to be lost, the next to go are the farmers and the ranchers. "They leave the land in droves," said Savory. "It doesn't matter what the economics are; it's a biological-diversity problem. ... We've got to reverse this loss of biological diversity in order to save our farms, our ranches, our communities, our villages, our cities—our nations."

This reversal, Savory explained, must begin with some understanding of the interdependencies among soil, plants, and animals and how they evolved in unison. Describing our earlier understanding of these interdependencies, Savory said: "We didn't realize that animal behavior, plants, predators [including humans], time, seasonal rainfall, and microorganisms were in fact one indivisible whole. Take any part of it out, and the whole thing crumbles."

I see now that "stopping the madness," minimizing our farming activities for a season has been healing for the land, as well as for John and me. Waiting and watching have brought an end to a winter season of the soul, a season when I feared that the loss of our control over the land and over all of our resources would diminish us. Instead, this frozen season of waiting, limp handed, has produced a good measure of enrichment, much of it coming to us seemingly with little or no striving on our part, and with significantly less expense.

I wonder: Did our time of stripping down come to us as a consequence of our own actions and choices, because we tried to rely too heavily on strength and surety, on the "swift steeds" of convention, trying to farm in ways that are acceptable to man? Did we ignore what our own land was trying to tell us, thus hindering the provisional simplicity that springs from the complexity of the healing balances inherent in the land and in God's processes? It is a question I think about when I read these words of the prophet Isaiah's: " 'In returning and rest you shall be saved; in quietness and in trust shall be your strength.' And you would not, but you said, 'No! ... We will ride upon swift steeds,' therefore your pursuers shall be swift."

* * *

It is an evening in January, and John and I have just finished our chores of feeding horses, heifers, and cows. We walk through the herd at dusk, studying the amount of hay the cows have left over. We check to see which cows look full and which look as though they should have eaten more.

Though the temperature is only zero, the breeze is dead quiet, so the cattle are comfortable despite the cold air. A tinge of rose colors the eastern horizon, diffused light refracting from the sun setting in the west. A full moon shines from the northeastern sky. The cows are spread around the feeding area; some eat the scattered leftovers of second-cut alfalfa. Others rummage through the remains of round bales of sorghum sudan hay, while still others chew cured slough grass, which John brought for the cows to eat as well as to sleep in. As we walk amid the animals, we speak freely with each other once more concerning our future.

Indeed, the "way in the wilderness" seems to be opening; and we perceive, in part, the "rivers in the desert."

I hope again in the words of the Psalmist: "He turns a desert into pools of water, a parched land into springs of water, and there he lets the hungry dwell ... ."

SWEAT AND STEEL

2002

Horsetails of snow swirl up and race skittishly across the field each time a gust of wind sweeps the ground like a great, invisible broom. The wind has picked up since John and I hand-pitched our first wagonload of loose hay to feed to the cattle. We are now coming back from the field with our third load. Pete and Skeet, our big, grey horses, pull the loaded wagon at a walk away from the haystack and follow the contour of the Big Hill east of the farmyard. We are headed to a feeding ground near the tall cottonwoods ringing the farmstead. There the cattle can eat their hay in relative shelter from the cold, northwest wind.

The gusting breeze makes the midday temperature feel much more brutal than what the thermometer reads, which is zero degrees. John sits on the wagon's bench seat, while I sit near him, on the mounded hay. To shelter my face I wear a warm hood handmade from rough felt by a Montana sheep breeder. The stiff hood, crafted according to an old Icelandic design, has a protruding edge, which serves to deflect the wind and light sleet. But John, with only a thickly knitted cap pulled down over his ears, has no such luxury. The sleet clings in tiny, frozen clumps to his eyelashes, mustache, and beard, transforming his visage into a living image of winter.

I am exhausted from the pitching.

"What have we done!" I wonder to myself, studying my husband's face for signs of fatigue and secretly considering that my stomach muscles feel like mush.

A PRAYER FOR THE PRAIRIE

As the team pulls the loaded wagon around the western slope of the Big Hill, I can see the loose stacks of hay spread out around our land. We have counted them before: There are nearly 50 in all. John piled them up last summer using one of our old tractors dating from the 1950s. To make the piles the tractor is fitted with a large sweep, or bucker, at the front. By driving the tractor down a line of hay that's been raked into a windrow, the sweep, which has long teeth, pushes the hay into mounds. With the help of hydraulic cylinders, the sweep lifts the mound of hay skyward, making it possible to pile the mounds into a big stack of hay.

It was our plan, when we harvested the hay in this fashion last summer, that we would indeed feed it to the cattle by pitching it by hand from the stacks onto a hayrack pulled by the horses. We planned to pitch the hay off again in the winter-feeding pasture. Along with putting up the loose stacks, John harvested hay last summer by using an old machine to bale hay into 1,000-pound round bales.

Now, in the winter, we alternate between these two systems of feeding hay: One day we pitch hay by hand to the cattle; the next day John uses the team and his round-bale hauler to feed the herd, which numbers 80-some head in all.

On many of the days when we pitch hay by hand, we pitch on and pitch off three loads of alfalfa in the morning and two to three loads of wild hay or sorghum sudan in the afternoon. The pitching sessions each last about two hours. It is antiquated technology, this hand-pitching of hay. Putting hay up in loose stacks and pitching it by hand to the cattle in winter is a sharp contrast to the way most cattle producers do it these days: by using a highly mechanized system of harvesting hay with wheeled rakes, expensive round balers or hay choppers, and feeding the hay to the cattle with winter-worthy tractors equipped with convenient front-end loaders. There is also a sharp difference in investment costs between the two systems, a difference registering in the tens of thousands of dollars.

On this day when wind-swept snow dashes across the field in ghost-like wisps, John parks the rack on the leeward side of the stack. I clamber to the top and pry up one forkful of hay at a time, slinging it down on the rack. The airborne hay is helped along by the wind. John works closer to the base of the stack, peeling off hay from the sides. I sweat underneath my snowsuit and Icelandic hood. The hay seems stubborn, tangled in its bed, unwilling to be pried loose. My pitchfork feels unhandy. My muscles ache . . . and I wonder if we have gone too far in our efforts to strip cost from our production system; I wonder if we have gone too far in our pilgrimage toward a simpler, more basic process of work.

Yet we persevere. And each day that we ride the wagon out toward the haystacks to pitch on another load of hay, I consider this work from a fresh angle, like a scientist studying the makeup of a new-found molecule under a microscope. My husband, who does the greatest share of the work, points out that the stacks of hay have a character, a pattern. "Don't fight the hay," he says. "Figure out how each buckerful fits into the stack, and then take the stack apart in accordance with how it was built." Indeed, I begin to be able to see this pattern.

Then, we buy a different pitchfork for me: a four-tined fork for pitching hay instead of the five-tined manure fork I was using. The new fork feels handy.

It is on about the tenth day of pitching hay that I notice a difference in my joints when I jump down from the wagon to open a gate for the team. My knees have a bit of spring that I have missed keenly for a good while. My stomach muscles are regaining tone; it is the return of a measure of firmness for which I have longed. Indeed, we are doing a work that is returning a greater degree of fitness to our bodies. In a matter of days, I am forming a positive answer to my silent question: What have we done? I sense now that we are discovering a manual process that holds a wealth of good for our farm and for our bodies.

We work in complete acceptance of our labor; we expect the sweat and tired muscles, so we do not comment about them. I am the one most likely to complain, but not about the work. I complain, rather, about the poor food choices I may have made the day before, and how eating the wrong foods steals my energy. Because we accept and, indeed, embrace the work as a desired goal, we do not view it as a hardship. Because it is not a hardship, we do not blame each other for it. And we certainly do not blame Pete and Skeet, who, more often than not, work as diligently and calmly as we, seeming to perceive the needful practicality and worth of their work. We are four partners working together.

As the horses pull the wagon back and forth from the field, John and I talk. Most often John speaks of new ideas he has about managing the cattle or hay crops; a new idea about how to schedule grazing periods, for instance, in order to make the most effective use of a piece of land, in relationship to our production goals, moisture conditions, or the needs of plants and wildlife. He speaks, too, of new insights he has about how Pete and Skeet work, how he can better trim their feet, how adjusting the bit higher in Pete's mouth, for instance, seems to cause a more relaxed attitude in the spirited but personable gelding.

John's unleashing of ideas flies in the face of what I read in the popular farm press and of what I hear agricultural "professionals" tell me in the course of my interviews with them. The gist of what they say is this: Farmers should spend less time in physical labor and more time in management. Yet John's management ideas seem to spring from his physical labor. It is the same for me. Many days at hay-pitching time, I no sooner climb on the wagon than a flood of ideas swamps my brain. My words may have been frozen when I left the computer, but by the time I return the sentences and concepts are fluid once again.

Yet there is more, when I scrutinize under my mental microscope our newfound task of pitching hay. One day, as we ride silently together on the wagon toward the field, it occurs to me that John and I know each other better than I sometimes think. We both reserve a measure of what might be called emotional solitude in our most intimate conversations. Because of that, there are of course parts of us that are unknowable to the other. Yet, shared manual labor, and the talking it fosters, seem to expose a measure of the mystery.

John and I are not newcomers to working beside each physically. Over the years we have set our hands in unison to many tasks carved from the mold of manual labor. And so I wonder, as we ride together on the wagon, as I sit beside my mate, who seems both unknowable and yet—more often than not—a complex piece of my soul that once was missing: Have the years of working together with our hands and bodies caused us to know each other more intimately than words convey? Often, on return trips I sit beside John on the bench seat. The wagon bumps over a hole. I lean into John's shoulder, and he leans back. It is a moment among many, when words do not seem needful.

As more days of pitching hay go by, more ideas take shape, ideas for doing more work by hand or with horses. The simple methods of working using farm-generated, renewable sources of energy comprise a circle, elegant in its simplicity: The horses providing the energy needed to feed the cattle also provide part of the energy required to harvest the hay the cattle eat. The horses also contribute part of the energy needed to harvest hay to feed themselves in winter. The manure from the horses and cattle fertilizes the land, including our garden. The garden provides the nourishment John and I depend upon in order to generate the energy needed to pitch the hay pulled by the horses.

Though the hard work taxes our muscles, the pitching itself strengthens and energizes our bodies in ways that, in our convenience-driven age of labor-saving devices and machines, are becoming increasingly hard to come by outside of fitness centers. The weak, muscle-cramped body I have hauled away from my computer in past years, after spending long winter months of writing, all the while doing little physical work, tells me that such a sedentary lifestyle is not healthful. I have come to see that a lifestyle sparing me physical exertion will only bring poor health. It is clear to me that Jesus' injunction that we must lose our lives in order to gain them is a spiritual truth applying to life on various physical planes.

In *The Unsettling of America* author Wendell Berry describes the outcome of withholding our bodies from physical engagement with our world: "To fail to employ the body in this world at once for its own good and the good of the soul is to issue an invitation to disorder of the most serious kind. ... And it is clear to anyone who looks carefully at any crowd that we are wasting our bodies exactly as we are wasting our land. Our bodies are fat, weak, joyless, sickly, ugly, the virtual prey of the manufacturers of medicine and cosmetics. Our bodies have become marginal; they are growing useless like our 'marginal' land because we have less and less use for them. After the games and idle flourishes of modern youth, we use them only as shipping cartons to transport our brains and our few employable muscles back and forth to work."

If our modern, labor-saving age has caused us to ignore, yes, even demean physical labor, it has also brought an unprecedented time of freedom concerning our choices of tools by which we can accomplish work. As ecologist Allan Savory has said, in sum, we are gifted in this age because the progression of mankind's technology from simplicity to complexity has produced an incredibly wide range of tools from which to choose when we consider the most holistic means of accomplishing a task. This insight has caused John and me to include in our list of possible work instruments, our own bodies and the unseen flow of energy bringing movement to our limbs in the mornings. Like the dawn seeping into the eastern sky first as a dusk and then slowly dissolving into full-blown light has come the insight that to ignore our bodies as fine-tuned instruments of labor is to ignore a sacred provision from God.

Still, the insight seems fragile. When faced with choices concerning the various tools by which we might accomplish certain tasks, the options that come most quickly to mind seem to be those involving some machine or some complex technology producing a quick-fix result. "We have learned to be fascinated by the statistics of magnitude and power,"

Wendell Berry adds in *The Unsettling of America.* "There is apparently
no limit in sight, no end, and so it is no wonder that our minds, dizzy
with numbers, take refuge in a yearning for infinitudes of energy and
materials."

Indeed, I feel that this learning has in effect been bred into my
bones. I am the product of generations of farmers who have sought easier
and faster ways of working, ways of working that will spare our bodies
from direct engagement with the task at hand. In so very many ways I am
thankful to live in an age when we are able to choose between simple and
complex technologies. Yet because of our generations-long indoctrination
toward seeking the labor-saving technologies, the choosing of the simple,
labor-intensive methods as alternatives requires conscious thought and
discipline.

But the more John and I practice such discipline, the more
unexpected riches we discover, riches hiding in the commonplace, wealth
stashed away in the everyday. Work begun from a point of relative
weakness—hinging as it does upon only the labor that can be
accomplished by one feeling human body as opposed to an unfeeling
machine of much larger magnitude—turns powerful in its sum effect. We
sense a great freedom lying in wait as a result of this discovery.

Yet obtaining this freedom seems to require an ongoing conscious
pulling of the mind toward a state of humility, toward an expectant
mindfulness of God's provisions. It is so easy to minimize what God
provides. It is for this reason that I am intrigued by passages from the
Book of Nehemiah. The prophet writes about the Israelites' experiences
in the desert: "Thou didst give them bread from heaven for their hunger
and bring forth water for them from the rock for their thirst. ... But they
were not mindful of the wonders which thou didst perform among them;
but they stiffened their neck and appointed a leader to return to their
bondage in Egypt."

The manna from heaven surely did not seem to the Israelites like the
bread to which they had been accustomed in Egypt. Rather than rejoice

in the food God graciously provided, they perceived a lack. And as for the water coming from the rock? Well, it surely must not have seemed as sure and continuous a supply of water as a whole river full of water. God's provisions, requiring as they did, such a daily, case-by-case renewal, must have seemed tentative, requiring a daily expectancy, an ongoing hopefulness, for God permitted no excess of either water or food . . . but always a sufficiency. Through an acceptance of this sufficiency lay their freedom.

This spiritual law, that God's power is magnified through human weakness, is an undercurrent flowing beneath our endeavors, our hopes and aspirations, and surely, our work. What impact does it hold then, I often wonder, for the ways in which we work, for the strategies we use to accomplish a given job, for the tools we choose to perform a certain task? Is God providing infinite simplicity in tools, while we search instead for finite complexity? Does God provide work strategies in an artful, multicolored web of interconnections, while we seek work plans designed of heavy, black straight lines? Do we choose a sledge hammer when a feather will work?

In our study of the array of methods we can use to accomplish our work, John and I find ourselves, more and more, seeking ways to work using simple tools and interconnected strategies. The more we study such tactics, the more we see that we do not have to bear alone the burden of the work required to tend this farm and to bring forth food from its land. Increasingly, we see that the animals and the plants can play more of a helping role than we had earlier imagined. Pete and Skeet's work is obvious, of course. But the cows, too, contribute labor when they do more of the work of feeding themselves, reducing the amount of hay we have to harvest in the summer and haul to them in the winter. To help the cows help themselves John schedules the cows' grazing of various pastures so that some fields have standing grass in late fall and very early spring. Because the cows then graze in these pastures in late fall and early spring, our hay-feeding season is shortened.

We have a plan, too, to mimic the haying and feeding practices of a visionary young South Dakota rancher about whom I have written. In summer he uses an old tractor, much like ours, to push swaths of hay into small piles. In winter he lets the cows eat at the piles, limit-feeding them, so to speak, by using electric wire to fence the meadow into strips, letting the cows eat at only a few piles of hay at a time. In this way, the cattle feed themselves very well, letting the rancher save thousands of dollars he would otherwise spend if he baled his hay and hauled it to the cattle in winter, as many other ranchers do in northern South Dakota.

Some Saskatchewan ranchers use a similar system of feeding their cow herds. They simply swath their hay in summer and leave it lying in long windrows for the cattle to graze in winter. They report that their cattle will dig through a foot or more of snow to eat the swaths. Though these ranchers harvest an emergency supply of hay in round bales to feed to the cattle on days when cold winds prevent them from gazing in open fields, nevertheless, their swath-grazing system of feeding drastically reduces costly wear and tear on expensive machinery.

Another way John and I are experimenting with methods by which we can let our cows help us, is in the seeding of fields to alfalfa or grass. The field we seeded most recently to alfalfa, John first applied the alfalfa seed using a rented air-applicator to drift the tiny, fine alfalfa seeds over the ground. He applied the seed later in the spring, after the first flush of quack grass and weeds had sprung up. Typically, the next step would be to harrow the field using a tractor. But because the green plants growing in the field offered succulent grazing for the cows, John turned the herd into the field to graze the weeds and quack grass, letting their hooves duplicate the work that would otherwise be accomplished by the heavy prongs of the harrow pulled by the tractor. In this way, the cows not only helped us to "seed" the field, but their grazing also controlled the weeds.

Yet not all cows are created equal in their willingness to work, in their expectancy to forage and fend for themselves. Just as I sense a seeming in-bred tendency within myself to seek labor-saving, mechanized ways to work, today's farm animals, too, are forgetting how to work, forgetting how to care for themselves, as the wild animals who survive know intuitively how to care for themselves.

In domestic farm animals physical adaptability to natural environments and critical instincts for gathering food and caring for young are qualities becoming increasingly difficult to find in mainstream agriculture. It is hard to imagine today's modern dairy cow, for instance, surviving as a pioneer family's milk cow once survived on the open prairie. Cattle genetically "forget" how to forage when feed, vitamins, and mineral supplements are hauled to them continually for generations. Their genes "forget," too, how to protect them from parasites after generations of people controlling parasites for them by quick-fix parasiticides. Pigs, for instance, "forget" how to avoid lying on their babies after generations of birthing only in cramped crates where sows are cradled by bars preventing them from rolling over on their piglets.

But such gross ineptness and poor workmanship are not the animals' fault. Modern agricultural practices of selecting replacement stock based on what animals can produce rather than by what they can survive has served to erode livestock's genetic code for adaptability and endurance. Yes, indeed, modern farm animals produce much. But to do it, they require much, so much that farmers are hard-pressed to provide it any other way than by machines and costly supplements or medicines.

John and I have spent years searching for practical cows, cows who will take a happy attitude toward the work of foraging for their own food, and who will thrive in spite of a measure of adversity in weather, for instance. We were lucky to eventually find such cattle.

Daisy is my favorite of these core group of hardy, work-minded cows. As ranchers today breed for uniformity in their cattle of all sorts, Daisy's odd, flamboyant color pattern of red and white patches and streaks of roan makes her undesirable. Her undesirability in the modern marketplace—since she might, heaven forbid, produce a feedlot steer with as bright a hide as she—is an ironic twist considering Daisy's keen survivalist instincts and physical abilities. Always in good flesh in spite of producing enough milk to wean a heavy calf in fall, Daisy is a determined grazer. Tips of buckbrush, flower heads of Canada thistles, vines of creeping jenny, and even a few broad heads of milkweeds, Daisy eats these plants willingly along with the choice grasses. Her workmanlike attitude toward grazing makes her a weed-control expert extraordinaire. On top of this, her walk is strong and true, not unlike the determined stride of a good horse. Because walking comes easy to Daisy, she willingly covers more ground in her search for nutritious forages to eat.

Indeed, animals working in partnership with plants can shoulder a surprising load of farm work effectively, reducing the need for costly, invasive and "labor-saving" technology. In his paper "Feeding the Village First," Fred Kirschenmann, director of the Leopold Center for Sustainable Agriculture, writes: "If we managed our farms by ... ecological principles they would look very different from the industrial farms that now dominate the landscape. ... we would have more moderate-sized diversified farms which grow five or more crops and have two or more animal species. The crop and livestock systems would be fully integrated. The waste from the cropping systems would be fed to the livestock and the wastes from the livestock would be used to fertilize the crops. In some locations crops and livestock would both be rotated through the system. In other locations, due to the ecology of the land, livestock would be grazed on native prairie and crops would be grown in the 'niches' of the prairie landscape. In all cases the diversity would keep diseases in check and provide for natural habitat that would harbor the species that help control insect pests. ... In other words a farm would be a production system in which nature's own ecosystem services would provide the majority of the fertility and pest and disease control that optimizes production."

Even weeds, which we farmers have learned to disdain so highly, have work to do. In his book *Holistic Management* Allan Savory writes:

"What we call weeds should not be blamed for stealing water and nutrients from our crops, but valued for the diversity they contribute, including the insects and microorganisms they attract. This added complexity offers protection against the few insects or microorganisms that actually damage crops or cause disease. All too often we reduce this complexity in our croplands for no good reason."

John has told me as much about the weeds in my garden. For whatever reasons—and I have a host of "excuses"—my garden grows a lot of weeds. Yet it also yields a lot of food. And what seems an ongoing miracle to me is that the plants are so seldom diseased or devastated by insects. I worry a bit when I hear neighbors complaining about the slugs, bugs, and blights damaging their garden crops. Each time I hear such stories of disaster, I wonder to myself, *when are these problems going to get out of hand in our own garden?* Yet so far it has escaped, and each year we have been blessed with a harvest providing us with more food than we can eat. John tells me this bounty results in part because the weeds add greater diversity to the garden, and with the diversity, as Savory says, come protection against disease and protection from the excess feeding of insects.

Of course, garden plants cannot compete neck and neck with weeds. They need, at the very least, a comparative advantage in growth. Until more natural weed-control processes result from our rotation, I work hard to give my plants an early advantage over weeds by hoeing, tilling, and hand-weeding as much as I can.

One year, concerned for his wife, wondering if my work in the garden was too hard, John suggested that we buy a ride-on tiller for me to use to control the weeds. But it is incomprehensible to me to share the time in my garden with a muttering machine. I can no longer imagine accomplishing the work of controlling weeds through any other means than by the use of my own hands and through the direct engagement of my muscles with simple tools: a hand hoe and two wheel hoes.

I find great freedom and simplicity in such methods of work. In the absence of unnatural noise I hear subtle sounds that would otherwise be drowned: the hoarse call of a rooster pheasant, leaves of corn rustling in the breeze. Because my wooden-handled tools are simply extensions of my own body, the tools stop when I stop, and the muffled sound of the blades scuffling through the soil ceases.

When I stop to rest, I take stock of the work: The rows of beans are tilled and the weeds, severed just below the surface of the soil, lie on top of the ground between the rows, covering the soil with a light residue of plant material. The residue shades the soil, serving as a mulch that hinders moisture from evaporating. On the far side of the corn, a couple of rows of peas remain to be tilled, and the young carrots need to be hand-weeded within the rows.

Though work awaits, the distant view beckons. To the west the Dog Den Butte juts up from the horizon. Grey light shrouds the butte, which marks the end of a hogback of distant hills ringing the southern horizon. The ring of hills begins in the east and circles around to the south, ending with the Dog Den due west of our farm.

Sometimes, after a break, it is hard to continue the work. My muscles often ache, of course. And some days a greyness of spirit causes the work to seem harder than it actually is. Still, my own will causes me to lean back into the handles of the wheel hoe once more, shoving the twin-bladed tool down the row of peas until the sweat runs down my neck and my back muscles burn.

But dogged perserverance brings rewards. The harnessing of my body to the physical labor almost always yields a triumph, and I come away from the work lighter in step as well as in spirit.

Yet another transformation occurs: In the midst of the struggle, at the point of greatest weakness of body and spirit, I sense a prayer forming. Sometimes it is conscious. At other times it is unconscious, shaped merely by a mindfulness of working in the presence of God. I have often felt too harried to pray consciously. But while at some physical task, I have thought to God: "Let my work be a prayer." I take hope from the theology of Brother Lawrence, a 17th century French monk who believed that the sum effect of such prayers equals those said on our knees. Though at first he despised the work, Brother Lawrence came to consider his time spent doing menial labor in the monastery's kitchen to be an important time of prayer, serving to draw him into the presence of God.

Such thinking holds great impact for manual labor, requiring as it so often does a sacrifice, an investment of sweat and discipline into thoughts that we can, by will, turn toward heaven. Indeed, the concept of work as prayer lends honor to physical labor and insight into the biblical proverb, "The work of a man's hand comes back to him."

Surely, then, beads of sweat offered to God in joy, hope, and expectancy can forge an outcome greater than steel.

A SACRED PACT

2002

As I park the car outside the gate to the pasture, I notice the tip
of a thunderhead building along the western skyline. It was not
there when I left home. But it is not surprising that a storm should brew
from this weather. The day is muggy and still, with a sweltering
temperature in the mid-90s. I set off to check the cows on foot anyway,
anxious to immerse myself in this place of shallow, blue lakes and rolling
hills of native prairie and fields once farmed but long since reseeded to
grass.

This is the grassland where we graze most of our cows in summer. It
is part of the land once farmed by my grandparents and still remains in
the ownership of extended family. It is the place where my father spent
his youth and much of the sweat of his young adult years, since he didn't
leave home until he was 27, when he married my mother in 1935. This is
a place where I too spent some of the sweat of my youth, since my
mother grazed cattle here all the years I was growing up. As I stride down
the trail to the west, I pass the spot where, nearly 40 years ago, I helped
my sister Karen and my brother John build a roughshod barbed wire
enclosure for capturing cattle. I was so small I was probably no help at
all. More of a hindrance actually, since I recall cutting my finger deeply
on a barb, leaving a scar that yet remains.

Farther down the trail I pass the spot where a wooden fence brace
once stood, completely removed now by renters who managed the land

between the time that I left my family's farm when I was 25, up until this year, the first year that the land has come under the management of my husband, John, and me. I built the brace that is now missing after I grew up, after my brother John and Karen left home.

I recall that on the day of its building, the weather was not unlike this: hot and dry. I dug the holes for the posts by hand with a posthole digger. After setting them in the holes and tamping them solidly into place, I fitted a wooden crosspiece between the posts. Then I braced them with two diagonal strands of barbed wire twisted together. I used the structure to anchor and stretch tight the barbed wires of the crossfence that once ran down the slope to the north. I worked alone, in solitude, surrounded by the silence I have come to know so well in these hills. It is a silence sometimes brimming with sound, especially at dusk in midsummer, when the voices of frogs, crickets, and shorebirds combine to create a blanket of sound that shapes the peculiar silence of a hill-scape solitude.

Now, nearly 25 years later, the work of my hands has indeed disappeared. Yet the familiar solitude remains, unchanged. I follow the trail, comprising only two tire tracks worn into the sod. The trail passes over the crown of a hill and down again, bending around a quiet, tree-ringed lake on the left. To the right, nestled at the base of a rise are the cement walls of a small barn, remnants of a homestead. The north wall of the barn has already fallen. In time the coarse, earth-toned cement will meld into the very soil of the slope, leaving no sign of the people who once called this spot their home, just as there is barely a trace of the native people who once lived out their lives on this land. Already the brown walls of the old barn seem merely an extension of the summer-browned crested wheatgrass growing all around.

Still farther on, the trail curves again around a lake; this one is on the right with a long sandbar where pelicans gather. To the southwest of the trail, along the gentle slope of hill, I see the brown heads of purple coneflowers, or echinacea, peppering the grass. This is the thick patch I'd hoped to find during my search for the cattle, and I place the container I have brought from home down on the ground beside the trail, where I'll pick it up again on my walk back. I plan to pick the health-boosting echinacea and brew a medicinal tea from the leaves when I get home. I will not take the heads or roots of the plants, only the leaves. Since I am picking these just before the late-summer weather withers them into crisp, brown curls, I reason that this harvesting method, of taking only the leaves just before they are about to dry out naturally, does not harm the plant, since the light-gathering abilities of the leaves have run their course for the summer, and the seed head has set and dried.

I am almost desperate for the echinacea tea. From a point of high energy earlier in the summer, my body and spirits have fallen into some peculiar malaise that leaves me chronically exhausted and pain-ridden. My intuition tells me the illness comes from my own doing, the result of unwise choices relating to work and a bout of discouragement. Because I have chained myself to my computer and a market garden nearly the entire summer, I feel as if I have hardly visited this land much at all since it came under our management. Now, I have come here in search of a cure; I seek the seed of a healing. It is not just the echinacea that I need. I need total freedom. I need to dissolve my spirit into this place, letting the steadfastness of the hills and the strength of the enduring prairie grass filter through my soul. And so, despite the heat and despite the pain at the top of my ribs, I walk on briskly, breathing in the clear air, determined to regain my strength.

Beyond the echinacea patch, I pick up a side trail, which follows a long ridge running north and south between two lakes and which eventually leads to a point where my grandparents' farmstead comes into full view. The buildings, situated barely a quarter of a mile away across a narrow lake, have stood empty for decades. To the west, beyond the buildings, the thunderhead now looms. It has grown quickly into a mountain of ominous, dark cloud, obviously moving due east. Now I feel uneasy, wondering if I will have enough time to hike the two miles or so back to the car before the storm strikes. From this vantage point, too, I finally spot the cows. They are grazing underneath the trees along the lake's edge.

Then, as I study the view in all directions, I see an animal that is out of place. Due east, across the lake on my right, one of our black-and-white Holstein steers grazes outside the pasture fence. If I don't get the steer back inside the fence, I reason, he could wander off and get mixed in with the neighbor's cattle. He might also tempt some of our other cattle to crawl through the fence, or walk around the end of the fence where it juts down into the lake east of the ridge. The problem is: I cannot get at the steer from where I stand since a lake separates us. Indeed, I could reach him by retracing my steps and going around the lake east of the ridge. But it would take more than three miles of hiking. The pending storm and my own spent endurance suggest hiking around the lake is not a practical option. *If you had more courage, you would simply walk across the lake where the cattle cross*, I think to myself. But the crossing seems wide; I do not know how deep the water is, and I have always been afraid of water.

Take your cues from the cattle; they wouldn't cross repeatedly at a point where the water is extremely deep or where the footing is treacherous, I reason. Fighting an inner war between fear and reason, I walk down the slope and stand at the edge of the crossing, studying the water, which, though it looks blue from a distance is indeed, upon close inspection, a murky slate-grey. The water carries bits of algae and sediment from the lake bottom, which is made more from soil than sand. Standing at the lake's edge, feeling faint and useless, I recall a family story involving one of my uncles: During his youth, when farmsteads now vacant were filled with families, the young people made it a pastime to swim in a deep lake south of here, on a farm known as Moorhead Number Three, since it was one of three farms owned by an investor by the name of Moorhead. One Sunday afternoon a young man was near drowning in the lake at Moorehead Number Three, but my uncle dove into the water and saved him.

My uncle must have been comfortable with the water because he understood it. He understood its nature, and knew how to read its moods. And he understood it, was familiar with it, because, like my father, he lived intimately with it, joining with the land and water in work as well as in play. He lived in an intimate relationship with this land of hills and lakes. His life and work were cradled by this place.

Then, as I stand at the water's edge, a calmness creeps over me; an insight dawns, and I think to myself, *It is a completely natural act to walk across this shallow lake.*

And so, I take off my shoes and socks and wade across the water.

* * *

What grows increasingly apparent to John and me is the fact that we live in a potentially dynamic and intimate relationship with the land, bound by a code of conduct resembling a marriage ethic. Distilled to its essence, my view of this marriage ethic as it relates to my union with John is this: That we are, ideally, two people jointly evolving into the sum total of God's vision for us, developing the strengths and fulfilling the potentialities God has placed inside us, as well as accomplishing the work He has marked for us to do.

Ideally, our relationship with the land we manage is a parallel, causing us to be honor bound to play a facilitating role in helping our spot of land to develop, or at the very least, maintain the strengths or potentialities with which it has been endowed by God. In return, we can expect treatment in kind from the land.

John and I have learned that our personal health is the most dramatic proving ground of this interdependent relationship. When we took over the management of the farm 12 years ago, we did not expect to grow our food from our own soil. Aside from the garden-grown vegetables my sister shared with us, we purchased vegetables from the store as well as some heavily processed foods. Believing our diet needed to be fortified, we sometimes purchased vitamin and mineral supplements. My aches were many, so I bought pills to relieve the pain. As the years passed, my pains increased, and my energy lagged, to the point where a medical practitioner prescribed a thyroid supplement.

But our habits and expectations relating to food evolved as new thoughts caused us to look more to our own place for health. All the while we experimented with and refined the work habits and practices needed to grow and store a year's worth of diverse vegetables from the garden. We harvested beef from our own cattle, animals that have consumed only forages, most of which are grown on our own land. We began avoiding processed foods almost completely. And we have experimented with wild plants, eventually weaving weeds like dandelions, sow thistles, and lamb's-quarters into our regular summer diet. Indeed, I now find the taste of domestic greens from the garden to be bland, compared to the zing of a sow thistle salad. Literature reports that many of these wild plants support health in specific ways. Dandelion greens, for instance, are reputed to promote liver health. Alfalfa, from which we make tea, helps to detoxify the body and eases inflammation, according to some sources.

We look to wild plants, too, for medicinal supplements, such as echinacea, of course, and also rose hips, which are the cranberry red, pea-sized fruit of the prairie rose. Rose hips, high in vitamin C, help fight colds and other infections. We've experimented, too, with catnip, willow bark, and hawthorn berries.

We learned how to make yogurt from goat's milk and yeastless, organic breads from flax meal and barley or rye flour. We learned that rotating a variety of grains into our diet, reducing and sometimes avoiding a daily consumption of wheat, reduced symptoms of allergies as well as joint pain. Indeed, the reduction in pain has been dramatic for me in particular. Taking a painkiller has, of late, been more the exception than the rule, breaking up a season of near-chronic pain lasting 17 years. The sum effect has been a sustained level of energy, so that I have—for the past year and a half—even been able to discontinue the thyroid supplement. Indeed, I now believe that I could have emotionally withstood to a much greater effectiveness the most difficult years of our financial stripping down had I not allowed my body to slip into a nutritional deficit.

I would never have known what this level of health actually felt like if I had not eaten this, more natural diet for a year or longer. It seems very nearly a discovery of renewed life itself. I cannot imagine returning to a full-time diet of conventional, processed foods. When we do in fact happen to eat meals made from such foods several times in a row, my energy lags, and both of us feel joint pain and allergic symptoms reappearing. The sum effect of the changes we've made in our diet and the sourcing of our food has so powerful an effect on our well-being that it is, I often think, like stumbling upon a secret chamber in the labyrinth that is our health—and all the myriad sensations and ebbs and flows in energy attending it—and discovering that, within this chamber are the keys to a profound bodily well-being.

According to Sally Fallon, a Washington, D.C., nutrition author and speaker, a nutrient-dense diet of foods produced by natural methods can indeed alleviate many health problems. "A health crisis has crept upon us so gradually we have forgotten that our estate—our heritage—is to have perfect health," Fallon told me in an interview. "None of us should need glasses; none of us should need to have our teeth straightened; none of us should have arthritis; and none should feel depressed. These are examples of bad health that occurs as the diet deteriorates."

Though we live in a time when serious illnesses are becoming increasingly treatable, Fallon, author of *Nourishing Traditions: The Cookbook That Challenges Politically Correct Nutrition and the Diet Dictocrats*, believes our medical technological advancements mask the fact that disease rates are alarmingly high. "I consider it a health crisis when we have epidemics in asthma, obesity, arthritis, and learning disabilities," she said. "It is a health crisis when one person in three is expected to get cancer, and when nearly one of every two people suffers from heart disease."

In her seminars, Fallon, who has spent years researching nutrition, shows participants how to take the diets they enjoy and transform them into nutrient-dense diets, packed with minerals and key nutrients. Fallon, who advocates purchasing as much food as possible directly from a farm, said: "We rob ourselves nutritionally when we choose foods from the center of the supermarket—the heavily processed foods such as extruded breakfast cereals, sauce mixes, foods based on partially hydrogenated vegetable oils, hydrolyzed protein, and those containing a lot of sugar and white flour, as well as artificial flavorings and MSG—monosodium glutamate. Pills, powders, and vitamins are no substitute for food either. They can be used as supplements, but your body wants food. Food contains nutritional co-factors that your body needs. Food also supplies nutrients in ways permitting our bodies to use them most easily. There is simply no substitute for nutrient-dense food."

Nutrient-dense foods do not simply happen. They are the gifts of sun, air, water, and nutrient-dense soil. And so, in my garden, as I bend over the tiny carrot seedlings, lifting the equally tiny weeds from their beds beside the carrots, my fingers stir the soil lightly. It is this soil, acting as God's agent, that has restored to me my health, and I am incredibly thankful. The soil helps me to become all that I can be, for greater health has brought me sustained energy, lighter spirits, and what I sense to be a more creative mind than what I once possessed. All these gifts join together to help me strive to work and live—and indeed pray and think—I hope, more productively. In sum, this soil sustains my life, and indeed, a high quality of life it is.

For such an indispensible life's partner, what then should be my response? If this soil is indeed giving me the foundation I need to become everything God envisioned me to become, to do the work for which He has marked me, then what gift do I give in return? How do I fulfill my role in this sacred pact with our soil?

To know it and to become intimate with it, to understand it seems to be the first and foremost need. Yet this knowing must leave room for mystery. And surely it must accommodate a measure of humility, accepting that this process of increasing familiarity acknowledges that a measure of unknowableness is present in my relationship with the soil, just as I acknowledge that a measure of unknowableness exists in my relationship with my husband.

Above all, to know the soil is to know that it is filled with life. But the full nature and scope of this life is the point of mystery. In his book, *Holistic Management*, ecologist Allan Savory writes: "Precisely what is taking place in any community at any one time is currently beyond human understanding and may always remain so. It is only relatively recently with the invention of high-power electron microscopes, that up to a billion or more organisms were found to be present in a cubic inch of soil or a spoonful of water. Most of these organisms have not even been named, and their relationships to one another and how they function within a community of organisms, which is far more important, is barely understood and difficult to imagine."

Knowing that the soil teems with life—most of which we do not even understand—causes John and me to study and question the ways in which we treat the soil. To preserve and indeed enhance this full volume of life within the soil causes us to experiment with growing practices that reduce tillage and eliminate the need for chemicals. Allan Savory describes how these practices can harm soils: "On farms, agricultural chemicals may temporarily help to produce higher crop yields, but destroy many soil organisms and inhibit others, such as those that fix nitrogen from the atmosphere. The net result is the destruction of soil, something humans cannot afford to do. Turning over deeper soil layers, as we do when plowing, leads to the breakdown of organic material and destroys millions of soil organisms. The planting of crops as monocultures results in a less diverse root system and an environment that discourages diversity in microorganism species. All the same problems and possibilities for damaging soils and mineral cycles also exist on rangelands and in forests."

It is John's goal that the land-management practices he chooses will contribute in some way to soil health and the improvement of its functions. Part and parcel of his aim is the estabishment of a diverse plant community on our farm. Not only does diversity of plant life have a healthful effect on soil but, as we have seen with our own diets, plant diversity is healthful also for own bodies, thus helping us produce physical work in large volumes with relative ease.

Common sense says, then, that a diversity in plants grown from healthful soil also contributes to the well-being of the animals grazing such plants. And, of course, the urine and manure produced by the animals is returned to the soil, strengthening it further.

Thus, the animals participate in the sacred pact we share with our soil. Indeed, their participation is of great importance to the overall prosperity of this pact. If the cows' workmanlike attitude is intact, for instance, they will graze the full spectrum of the diverse plants growing in their pastures. Because the diversity springs from and builds upon increasing health in the soil and plant community, the plants the cattle graze are more nutritious in themselves. Thus, the health of the cattle increases, causing their innate workmanlike tendencies to grow so that they seek even more aggressively diverse plants to graze. The same principles hold true for our horses, who are a major source of power for this farm. Increasing levels of soil health with its resultant increases in plant health and diversity cause increased health in the horses. This strengthens their ability to shoulder their workload with a minimum of effort.

Yet John and I have surely made many mistakes in the treatment of the soil. How could it be otherwise, considering that there is much we do not understand about soil life, as Allan Savory says. Much of our work then, with plants and soil comprises a cautious experiment, requiring much study and careful observation of the effects of our work upon plants and soil life. Such study requires us to develop the habit of looking down at the soil and its immediate plants, rather than across, as people typically look across a field or an entire landscape. Though we have looked down at our soil for nearly as long as we have been farming, John and I are learners at looking down. I don't believe that will ever change. For there is so much to see, so many connections to make. So many changes to note.

And as we look down, and wait, and watch, and study, it seems that I see a mysterious, beautiful pattern emerging from our interactions with the land. It is as if God has choreographed the ebbs and flows of our economic conditions into a graceful dance with the ebbs and flows of His plants. The sum effect is increased health for the land.

A pasture north of our farm serves as a striking example of this choreography, in which John's hard work and willingness to study plants played a role: Twelve years ago, when we first took over the farm, the pasture we call the South Railroad Pasture produced a scant, slow-growing harvest of bromegrass and quack grass. When we looked down at it, there were inch to an inch-and-a-half bare spots between the grass plants, and the soil looked grey brown in color. Then we began grazing a lot of cattle in the pasture for short periods of time, giving the pasture long rests in between grazings. Slowly, in response to such grazing, the grass populations began strengthening. Some of this extra grass formed a thatch, covering the bare spots between plants and providing shade, thus minimizing the loss of moisture due to evaporation.

But then came the couple of years when we had no cattle, and we did not graze the pasture. One year happened to be the year that weather and moisture conspired to bring a flush of volunteer sweet clover from the earth. Germinating from seeds that had lain dormant in the soil probably for years, the clover covered the entire pasture. It set seed that fall and regrew the next summer. The clover fixed nitrogen in the soil, and the following year the grass boomed. A greater diversity in grass varieties has appeared, helping the ground thatch to fill in the spaces between the plants. The net effect has been a tremendous increase in the productivity of the pasture.

John and I still walk there, looking down, marveling at the changes that have transpired in the plants. Usually, we walk beyond the pasture, crossing the railroad and exploring, too, the grassland north of the tracks. The walk is likely to take us to Sand Lake, where we stand on the shoreline and look out across the shimmering water. We take a different path on the walk home, inspecting our fields, looking down, finding as many problems as successes. In an unused strip of grass along the north edge of the Eighty we see that the grass population is declining and bare patches of earth are being exposed due to a lack of grazing or any other type of harvesting.

Walking farther south, we come to the gumbo lowland where alkaline soils predominate. John tells me he plans to broadcast seeds of alsike clover in this corner of the field, where the cows graze. The clover should work to neutralize the alkalinity of the soil, he says. Then, the notion strikes him to check the Canada thistle patch in the paddock running along the lowland just west of the Big Hill. So we head east, hiking across the alfalfa field, past the big slough with the Lunch Tree, where we ate our sandwiches at noon the first summer we worked together on this land. It was the year the whole farm grew nothing but quack grass, and we cut all the grass for hay.

When we reach the paddock with the thistle patch in it, we find that, indeed, the cows have eaten many of the flower heads and tips of the prickly plants. Their hooves have also trod down and otherwise damaged many of the plants. We had hoped this would happen.

One more idea strikes us, and we slip under the paddock wire, walking up the slope of the Big Hill. The slope is sandy; that's one reason John planted it to alfalfa a couple of years ago. Though the plant population is thick, the plants are shorter and more yellow near the top of the hill. John has never tilled across the top of the hill, where the soil is the most fragile. So the hilltop remains covered with its cloak of quack grass, dandelions, and volunteer sweet clover that grew there when we first came to the farm. Kneeling down in the alfalfa, John opens his jackknife and sinks it into the earth, prying several inches of soil loose. The particles are fine and sand-like. If they were thicker, more crumb-like, they would be healthier. "We need to haul some compost across this slope," he says.

His eyes are ever searching for even the smallest of ways to help heal what illnesses are present in our land. Yet healing is a slow process; progress seems snail-like, and the results of our attempts at healing hard to read. But slow results do not deter him. I have learned, over time, that my husband's spirit is bound to do what he believes is best for the life living in the soil, regardless of economics and other external factors. He acts on good faith.

The sacred pact between this man and the land epitomizes the challenge author Tom Sine poses in his book *Wild Hope*: "In the bibilical story, the creation is seen as innately sacred because God created it. It is pervaded by the presence and the purposes of the living God. Christ became a part of it, and God intends to redeem it. If we choose to embrace the biblical vision of a world made new, therefore, we must also commit ourselves to developing a new sense of reverence for all created life. We must be in the forefront of those working for the restoration of the created order."

A BETTER LIFE

2002

(The introduction to this chapter is adapted from a fictionalized historical account included in an article published by *North Dakota LIVING*, previously the *North Dakota REC/RTC Magazine*.)

Orange and bronze light spilled across the western horizon as Charlie MacDonald and his companion broke camp near Middle Station, mounted their horses and set off to the west, the last light of day barely showing the way. Wary and silent, the two mail carriers nudged their lean horses into a swinging jog; the pack mule tied to MacDonald's saddle dragged back on his halter for the first few paces, and then picked up the stride.

Following ravines and sidehills, the pair traveled a spell up a gradual incline. The summit showed the full expanse of the western horizon. Sheltered on both sides by rolling terrain, the two pulled up and sat silently in their saddles, scanning the dark outlines of the hills in the distance for any sign of movement, any sign of camp-fire smoke. As the last bronze hues of the sun melded into the curve of the earth, the dim outline of the Dog Den, a rounded promontory some 20 miles to the west, marked the travelers' way. They would aim to pass two or three miles to the south of the butte's base.

It was October 1867. That summer U.S. infantry troops had established Fort Stevenson along the Missouri River and Fort Totten near Devils Lake in northern Dakota Territory. Mail and military directives passing between the facilities were carried by such ingenious frontiersmen as MacDonald and his companion, employees of a government mail contractor at Fort Totten. MacDonald had been hired on in August as chief guide of the couriers between the forts. Like most other mail carriers, he was of Native American and Caucasian descent and from the Canadian Red River region.

Steeped in the survivalist skills of a fur-trading culture, MacDonald possessed an uncanny sense of direction. His keen memory and acute powers of observation drew even the smallest landmarks along the trail into sharp focus, enabling him to travel easily at night. During the few months of his employ MacDonald had already displayed a bent for choosing horses that could handle the hazards of prairie travel. His favorite mount was cool-headed but alert, an agile-striding creature whose footing was sure—even in the dark.

As the two mail carriers sat in the shallow draw, waiting for deeper darkness before crossing the flat plain before them, the otherwise dauntless MacDonald studied the Dog Den with unease. For a reason he couldn't quite fathom, the landmark—named by the tribes of the region "The Mountain That Looks"—had filled him with trepidation from the first day he'd seen it. True, he reasoned, the butte's deep, wooded ravines harbored warriors trying to protect their land from the invasion of the whites. Many of them acted in opposition to the decisions already made by higher chiefs, who had made peace agreements with the forts. It was this danger that caused the mail carriers to travel by night. Still, something else about the sight of the Dog Den fueled MacDonald's remorse . . . something like the sense of being caught up in a great, reeling storm cloud reaching from heaven to earth, wreaking destruction across the plains, down the ravines, and over the hills . . . and in its wake changing the native people and the nature of the prairies forever.

MacDonald shook his head, casting the uneasy feeling aside. With a glance, he signaled his companion forward, and the two continued their trek west. A half-moon lit the southern sky; cranes called overhead. And in the last, dim light of the setting sun, slate-grey clouds hung like funeral shrouds above the crest of the Dog Den.

* * *

The trail the two riders followed more than a century ago was only a segment of a long, overland route just coming into use. Laid out by earlier military explorations, the overland route connected St. Paul, Minn., with Fort Peck and Fort Benton in Montana and, eventually, with the gold fields that had opened up around Great Falls. The segment of the trail traveled by the mail carriers that night was also used by wagon trains carrying supplies between the forts. Indeed, one military record reports that wagon trains comprising as many as 110 or 120 wagons pulled by oxen passed back and forth between Fort Stevenson and Fort Totten. It was the steel-rimmed wooden wheels of the creaking freight wagons that carved the trail into the sod.

Change stations for the mail were established at points along the trail already known to be camping spots because of the presence of spring water and shelter. Mail carriers traveling between Fort Stevenson and Fort Totten, for instance, met at a point called Middle Station, located in the northern part of what is now Sheridan County. Today, two towering cottonwoods growing on the edge of a spring mark the spot where the camp was located. The trees are situated about a quarter of a mile beyond the boundary of a pasture on my grandparents' farm. Indeed, the well-rutted trail traveling through my grandparents' land from east to west is the old Fort Totten trail. The segment passing through the pasture was used by farm families for decades after the surrounding homesteads were settled in the early 1900s.

But a part of the trail heading due west from the twin cottonwoods never saw this later, extended use. Because of that, this short stretch of trail is hardly visible. The rutted tracks now leave barely discernable scars across the sod because the wounds carved by the wagon wheels have long since been healed over by the prairie. Only twin depressions in the grass slip silently up a gentle, pristine slope to the west of the spring where great numbers of oxen once watered—and where mail carriers and teamsters once washed their faces.

John and I visit this spot on foot sometimes. When I am in the presence of the looming cottonwoods, I sense the living that has gone on before me. And I sense, too, the tension, uncertainty, and indeed, desperation of a people in transition. I sense the steady, onerous rhythm of the American Dream marching west. It was a march that brought a widespread uprooting of the American Indians from the plains and a planting of the settlers in their place. For a season, the settlers and their children thrived, building farms from homesteads and bustling towns whose businesses serviced the farms.

But the American Dream has continued marching "west," long after the most remote reaches of the physical West were conquered. The Dream continues to march yet across the plains, traversing now on slick interstate highways and exhaust trails of jets piercing the once-pristine skies. Indeed, in the wake of these modern trails of the American Dream, the way of life on the prairies is changing again . . . dying again: Many farmsteads once filled with life are silent, save for the wind sighing through the broken window panes of looming old barns. In abandoned towns, like Lincoln Valley, the streets are overgrown now with grass. In such discarded villages the homes where people ate, slept, and loved are grey, broken skeletons crumbling into the back yards where gardens and flowers once grew. North Dakota farmer-poet Terry Jacobson writes of the meaning of this in his book *Crazy Musings from the North Outback*:

The buildings stand like tombstones
on a rural way of life
of neighbors and sharing
of community and caring
of hard work and strain,
slipping away into history,
robbing us of a way of life
as we build bigger farms
reducing farming to a business.

A PRAYER FOR THE PRAIRIE

The American Dream. It has seemed our salvation, the undergirding of a nation premised on limitless possibility for individuals, yet freedom for all. Sketch the Dream in familiar pictures, and we see images we have long honored: Thomas Edison inventing the lightbulb, the Wright Brothers careening through the air, and Abraham Lincoln walking from a small farm to the White House—admirable accomplishments of a people with drive and imagination. Yet when left unfettered and focused solely on self, when its motives and consequences go unexamined, the American Dream is insatiable, marching forward for no better reason than for the sake of marching forward. Author Tom Sine examines the societal impetus for this in his book *Wild Hope*:

"Undeniably, the Western Dream, modernization, and market-oriented economics have provided impressive material benefits. Even former Communist countries are belatedly acknowledging the superiority of the Western Dream and the market forces that drive it in terms of economic growth and the sheer capacity to produce enormous quantities of consumer goods. Nowhere has this dream proved more successful than in the United States ... .

"But to really understand this dream, it isn't enough to look at the pragmatic benefits; we must also look at the societal forces that drive it. The Western Dream is driven by the invented need for ever-increasing levels of stimulation.

"John Rader Platt, a professor of physics at the University of Chicago, [asserted] that in this modern era we have invented the fifth need of human kind. In addition to the basic survival needs of air, water, food, and protection from climatic changes, 'the fifth need is the need for novelty—the need throughout our waking life for continuous variety in the external stimulation of our eyes, ears, sense organs and all our nervous network.'

"Our indoctrination to crave novelty, begun early in the century, has stepped up its pace in recent decades. A constant onslaught of advertising has conditioned us, instead of restricting our consumption to those things we need, to increasingly expand our wants and embrace products we never even considered before. And the result is the creation of a society whose economic health depends on constantly increasing consumer appetites, not only in the United States but around the world. Of course, it is precisely those expanding appetites that are creating our mountains of garbage; threatening our air, water, and land; and undermining our spirituality.

"I believe the primary reason we have been seduced into becoming superconsumers," Sine continues, "is that we have bought into an image of the better future that equates happiness with acquistion. We have really come to believe that the more we accumulate in our garages, ring up on our charge cards, and invest in the newest novelties, the happier we will be ... . The powers have persuaded us as a culture that our ultimate human purpose is to become successful consumers."

Fueled by these forces the American Dream continues its trek "west," packing its bags, leaving the farms, and backing out of the driveways of tiny country towns and heading off for the city, where slick, shining superstores beckon, ensuring a constant supply of more things than are needful. Glimmering, super-supermarkets, for instance, offer the vast array of fresh produce and convenience foods that the little grocery stores on the Main Streets of our hometowns could never think of stocking. And if the food selections from the big supermarkets don't meet all nutritional needs, never mind. Sprawling pharmacies offer shelf after shelf of products designed to provide the nutrition that might be missing from the purchased food.

Even as these superstores thrive, their smaller counterparts in rural villages die for lack of trade. When the small businesses close, the jobs and needed services they once provided are gone, too. The people who worked at these businesses often leave town. As fewer and fewer people remain, other businesses suffer from the reduced trade, and schools and churches struggle to stay open. The loss of services and reduced diversity in social life redouble the temptation experienced by those remaining to seek a better life elsewhere. Many look to bigger cities to supply their groceries, clothing, hardware, and entertainment. A vicious circle results, causing the lifeblood of rural communities to drain into urban centers. Why should we be surprised, then, that the streets of some villages are now overgrown with grass, and the sidewalks are disappearing also in other hamlets?

Yet, of course, it is not only novelty and a seemingly endless array of products from which to choose that is luring many rural consumers away from their hometown shops. It is price, too. Cheap prices. Prices small, local businesses cannot compete with because the superstores depend on volume sales to make up their profits. In the supergrocery stores the cheap prices often reflect to an even greater degree than do the prices of small-town grocery stores, the influence of corporatization. Consumers—urbanites, small-town folk, and farmers alike—end up supporting the big-business system with their purchases. The vicious circle goes round, and in the end, many support the very system contributing to the low prices farmers receive for commodities, the low prices causing many family farmers to leave the land, renting or selling their land to larger producers—who become larger and larger in the process. In an interview for an article, North Dakota poet and organic farmer Terry Jacobson told me:

"[Consumers] have been seduced by cheapness. The corporations seduce us by making chickens, for example, so cheap that farmers can't afford to raise them for that low price. [Mass production makes many things] so cheap we have to have an exploitive system to produce them. We are seduced by bargain prices. We have gotten into the habit of trying to buy everything at the cheapest price rather than thinking about each of our buying decisions and asking ourselves: How does justice fit in here? What price is fair—for the farmer as well as for the local or smaller business?"

The exodus of both people and trade from our rural communities has, of course, been going on for decades. To a great extent, we rural people have lived in jealous eclipse of our city cousins, causing us to seek what they have. Our cultural past shows a thin veil of separatism between us. Some silent, mostly unspoken, generalized bias exists: that to be from the city is to be sophisticated and to be from the country is to be simple; to be from the city is to be cultured and to be from the country is to be uncultured. At its core it is, of course, a myth. But nevertheless the veil exists . . . because the bias is old and deeply entrenched. It is a subtle, unrecognized force causing many rural people to try to keep up with what "the Joneses" in the city are doing, and life's external trappings are often the yardstick.

If these external trappings slip into "peeling paint and broken glass," they signify "a way of life succumbing to an awful inevitability," as one newspaper editorial described the state of many of North Dakota's rural communities, after describing by comparison the thriving economy of one of our state's regional business centers. The editorial implied that "peeling paint and broken glass" diminish our standard of living, which the state's economic developers hold must be equal between rural and urban areas.

Yet, if standard of living is a term used to refer purely to economic conditions and external trappings of comfort or fiscal prosperity, I do not know then—beyond fulfilling the obvious needs of food, shelter, safety, and access to communication, education, and health care—what standard of living has to do with quality of life and spiritual fulfillment. Nevertheless, as Tom Sine states in *Wild Hope*, striving for a higher standard of living is a tendency deeply entrenched in our culture: "In the Western Dream, the better future has come to be seen as ever-increasing levels of economic growth, technological progress, and personal consumption."

And so, the sleek, shiny stores in the bigger cities beckon. Within their colorful, comfortable interiors the very experience of shopping is chic. Here, we don't have to be reminded that differences in "standard of living" exist between urban and rural communities. We don't have to be reminded that some of the buildings on the Main Streets of our hometowns need paint; that some roofs leak when it pours rain. Here, in these posh surroundings, people don't have to be reminded that some of the storefronts of Main Street buildings back home are boarded over. Here, in the superstores, we do not have to compare ourselves and what we are buying to the Joneses . . . for we have become the Joneses.

Yet, striving to emulate our city cousins in standard of living costs our rural communities much more than losses in sales revenue. It costs us our youth. This thin veil of bias between city and country is like a faint, barely visible film floating over the aspirations of rural young people. It blurs their view of the potential of the adult lives they might lead in a rural setting. The veil blocks their sight of the spiritual wealth they might uncover in a rural home if they set their hands to it. The spiritual wealth they could find if they worked at it with sincerity centers on mankind's deepest values concerning family, community, a sense of individual worth, heritage, traditions, creative silence, and working in concert with nature. But this potential wealth remains hidden from the view of many. And so the young people are inclined to leave, and the adults are inclined to encourage them to leave.

We here in rural communities have simply not celebrated enough the great treasure of our rural expressions of spirituality. Indeed, down through the generations, we have encouraged our children to seek "a better life" elsewhere. To be sure, some careers can only be best pursued from an urban setting. But many of those who have urged their children to seek "a better life" elsewhere, were they not, in many cases, focusing their eyes simply on the higher standard of living their children could gain by leaving?

* * *

I was one young person who never wanted to leave. Yet that is not to say that I did not, on some occasions, experience twinges of self-consciousness concerning my ruralness, in comparison to another person's urbanness. I recall a painful incident in which some city cousins came to visit us on the farm when I was a child. As we sat around our oak dining room table, my cousin, who was five or six years old, I think, read to us from the Bible. I went outside by myself soon after, troubled by the fact that, though I was younger, I could not read. Somehow, in my mind, this fact equated with the fact that I lived on a farm.

As I grew older, I noticed that my mother spoke of certain urban relatives as being refined. I never heard her refer to any rural people as being refined. Her focus tended to be on individuals' hands, that so-and-so had such refined hands, as if the appearance of their hands was a mirror of their intelligence, character, or temperament.

I must admit that the connotations I drew from my mother's observations caused me to feel defensive. For my hands were hardly refined. Indeed, they were thick from work, with hard, dark-brown calluses on the palms and scars from the bites of barbed wire fences. Yet I felt insulted at my own thought that I should have to apologize for my hands in defense of my intelligence or my character. Of course, my mother had no notion of my feelings and would have likely countered them if she had known. For she was, in sum, a champion of rural living; in one neighbor's estimation: "a hard-core rural person" in her determination to respect and support a way of life on the farm.

Ironically, after I married John and we began the work of tending the farm, the work-hardened features of my husband's hands drew her comments again. John's hands are callused on the palms, with the skin on the sides of his fingers thickened and prone to cracking. "They look just like Roy's," Mom often said wistfully, remembering my father's large, work-worn hands, with their thick, round thumbs. When she spoke of John's hands, the look of admiration filling her eyes said she clearly respected the worker, and the integrity and humility that often characterize those who use their hands in labor.

A PRAYER FOR THE PRAIRIE

Indeed, it was probably my mother's love of farm life, and of working with cattle and horses and other farm critters, like rabbits and chickens, that sparked my own intrigue. When I was a little girl, I played with a toy farm set more than I played with dolls. Any twinges of self-consciousness I might have felt in my youth relating to my ruralness never dampened my yearning to live and work on a farm. At an early age, when I thought about becoming a writer, it was always from the context of becoming a writer who was also a farmer or rancher.

My dreams persisted even in exciting, faraway settings. In 1969, when I was 16, Mom and I traveled to visit my sister, Karen, who was teaching in Ethiopia in the Peace Corps. On the way, we toured London, armed with the travelers' guidebook *Europe on $5 a Day*. After visiting Trafalgar Square, Hyde Park, and Buckingham Palace by day, we often talked of the farm by night. On that trip, my mother spoke enthusiastically about building a small feedlot, an enthusiasm that sparked my own imagination. Later on our trip, riding a train approaching Athens, Greece, I studied a hill-rimmed plain beyond the window, daydreams of cattle tugging at my imagination. Three years later, living for a few months outside of London and studying at a riding school set amid trees and winding village avenues, I longed for the prairie's wide-open vistas. I yearned to return to the farm.

Still, after college, I left for a time.

Then, when my husband, John, and I returned to run the farm in 1990, any preconceived notions I had about farming and a farming way of life based on previous experience were stripped away. John and I gradually discovered that the agricultural "rules" under which we had grown up, and under which we had both worked while employed at a large Canadian cattle ranch, could no longer guarantee economic success. The harder we tried to follow the old rules, the deeper we fell into a financial black hole. The disparity between the exorbitantly low prices we received for cattle and grain in relation to the exorbitantly high prices we paid for fuel, repairs, and supplies simply left no income and seemingly, no way of life.

For me, the revelation was cataclysmic. I had once stood at the summit of the majestic Acropolis in Athens, a visitor there by the strength of an income earned from a small family farm in North Dakota, an income to which my own hands had contributed their labor. Yet now, in my middle age, as a result of working on the very same farm, I had no money some days to buy gas to drive to town; sometimes John had no money even for bolts.

The loss of our future as farmers seemed imminent. Still, we survived and continued as people might who are struggling to climb from a deep well into which they have fallen: by digging their fingers into the ridges and crevices of the cribbing.

Yet somehow, in the well, light began to dawn, a distant glimmer of an insight. No solace, really, only the unveiling of thoughts. And an immersion in humility. We had come to the farm with the straightforward assumptions that we knew how to accomplish our goals. But our thinking was far too linear for the complex web we confronted here—a web comprising our unique finances, resources, and family relationships. Rather than straightforward accomplishments, what resulted instead from our work was a loss of control in almost every avenue of our lives.

Yet from the vantage point of humility, from the state of holding nothing in our hands, came the gradual insight that there was indeed a way out of this inscrutable well of paralysis. But we could see that the way out certainly did not lie along familiar paths. We needed an infusion of new thinking before we could find the way out. And so, for my part, to the best of my faltering ability, I laid my trust in God, believing the words of the prophet Isaiah: " ... your ears shall hear a word behind you, saying, 'This is the way, walk in it.' "

While working and while waiting for new insights, John and I opened our minds to the views of free-thinking writers such as Wendell Berry and Allan Savory. Piece by painfully slow piece came a vision for the farm-building strategy that we gradually came to believe would pull us from the inscrutable well and place our feet on solid ground.

I began to conceive of a healthy, just economic system as one in which individual farm and household economies such as ours comprised the most basic building blocks. These would join together with other healthy farm and household economies to form a foundation for the local economy, just as each local economy is then in turn a building block joined together with the blocks of other local economies to form the broader economy. So, I reasoned, if my home was economically unstable because it was buffeted continually by vicissitudes in the general economy such as job availability, wages, the price of groceries, and the cost of health insurance, never mind the spiraling-beyond-control costs of farm inputs, how could it contribute fully to a stable local economy? Our farm and household were wholly at the whim of each of these variables.

I began to conceive of each of these as enterprise centers; and that, if we could attain a good measure of control of each, we would become economically more stable. We would, in effect, fold each enterprise center, each variable, into our home and into our farm and capture our share of the economic activity from that enterprise center; in short, we would purchase our own production.

It has taken years for us to evolve closer to such a system for both farming and running a household. And there is so much more to be done. We need to further reduce our dependency on purchased items, and we need to phase out more of the financial demands requiring the immediate need for income earned off the farm. This could free more time and labor, allowing more of it to be invested in maximizing the economic potential hidden in each of our internal enterprise centers.

Yet what we have accomplished so far sometimes seems miraculous in terms of the magnitude of the impact it has had on increasing our health and in helping us to climb nearer the top of the economic well into which we had fallen. For example, I often envision that the food we grow on our land, along with the wild plants we harvest for both food and medicine, fold back into our home and farm our share of the broader economy's profits from the enterprise centers of food and drug processing, food and drug advertising, and food and drug retailing. Our reliance on horses to supply a large share of the power required to harvest hay and feed it to the cattle saves fuel, of course, not to mention the wear and tear on tractor engines. John's designing and manufacture of his own horse-drawn farm equipment folds back into the economy of our farm the profits the farm-equipment manufacturing industry would otherwise extract from us.

Self-reliance holds opportunities for local communities, too. In his paper "Feeding the Village First," North Dakota organic farmer Fred Kirschenmann, director of Iowa's Leopold Center for Sustainable Agriculture, describes the potential effects of such local self-reliance: "Feeding the village first is a concept which suggests that local community economies are healthiest when they are as self-reliant as possible, especially where food and agriculture are concerned. Self-reliant communities are healthiest because they are free to pursue their own course, shaped by cultural norms which evolved in those communities to maintain the local public good. ... when the economy of a local community or region is dependent on distant communities to supply its needs and buy its raw materials, then its own economy becomes extremely vulnerable to economic forces over which it has no control. ... We can, for example, see this principle at work as we watch the agricultural economy of North Daktoa collapse."

Because our growing self-reliance reduces the amount that we purchase as consumers, it could be construed, I suppose, that John and I are poor supporters of our local economy. Yet on the other hand, our growing self-reliance serves to stabilize us, helping us to be less prone to moving away from our local community because we can no longer afford to live here.

In yet another vein, because we are so busy operating each of our enterprise centers, we consider driving 60 miles to the nearest regional business center to shop for necessities to be too time-consuming. It is only one reason we treasure so greatly our local grocer, Bennie, who sells groceries as well as some hardware and vehicle repair items from his old Standard gas station building on the Main Street of Kief, only a mile and a half from our farm. From Bennie we can get most of what we need, like chore gloves; and some things that we don't need, like halvah and Greek olives. With only 13 people living in Kief and surrounded by a rural population that is few and far-flung, Bennie's store experiences long silences between customers. But that doesn't bother Bennie much, since the store is simply an addition to his home, as was the gas station and repair center he once operated.

In spite of the fact we grow nearly all of our own food, our bill at Bennie's always seems to add up to a significant sum. But we seldom quarrel with the amount. With the money we save from capitalizing on our own enterprise centers, we have a little more money with which to support key local businesses. When we shop at Bennie's, for instance, we can see so clearly where our money goes. We are part of an extended family, supporting each other. If we fail and move away, Bennie loses an important customer. If he closes his doors, the economy of our home and farm will be weakened because it will cost us more in time, fuel, and vehicle repairs to drive the eight extra miles to get to the next-nearest local grocer. But even more than that, I think, we support each other out of simple, genuine concern.

* * *

I walk some days to a wetland at the edge of one of our fields. Often when the sun sets, its golden rays spill across the land and tint the slough waters in amber tones—the color of fine wine. Young cottonwoods ring the slough. They sway gently to the rhythms of the breeze while the yellow-headed and red-winged blackbirds perching amid the bulrushes blend their voices in a joyful chorus. On such walks I am often overwhelmed by thankfulness for the opportunity we have to live and work on this farm, in this community of people. I do not think myself Pollyana-like for feeling so. I simply love living in concert with the land, in this sacred place where soil and water, farm animals and wildlife, insects and birds—and rain, wind, and snow conspire with the work of our hands.

I pray to God that we will have the wisdom to use this time we have here wisely. I hope that our farm can become, in time, a burgeoning garden where people, soil, plants, wildlife, and farm animals can thrive. I pray that it can become a place where God's version of prosperity reigns, not just in economics, but also in our spirituality, emotional health, personal relationships, connectedness to community, and physical health. Possibly my love of this life has deepened because of farming's difficulties, rather than in spite of them. Twelve years we have farmed, and for most of that period we have been economically stripped down. But this difficulty has masqueraded as a blessing, nudging our eyes away from the materialistic trappings of economic wealth, to our spiritual riches and a deepening faith.

GIFTS

FROM THE FARM

2002

(The short story introducing this chapter was previously published in *Western People* under the title "To the Land, With Love.")

Hand in hand, they walked along the winding path to the house. Neither spoke. It was a time to be quiet, a time to reflect. Their day's work was done; their animals were cared for. The stars hung low in the evening sky, and as they walked Joanna thought how diamond-like they shone. Their tiny, fiery lights fueled a warmth she felt somewhere deep inside. With Will's rough, calloused hand in hers, her spirit felt light. Life was as it should be.

When they reached the door to the house, Will opened it for his wife. But then he gently slipped his hand from hers and said softly, "I have to go now."

And the next moment he was gone, striding quickly down the path back to the barn.

As she awoke from her dream, Joanna's eyes focused on the familiar walnut dresser by the side of her bed. And as sleep gave ground to awareness, the old loneliness sifted over her until it lay like lead in the pit of her stomach. It was only a dream. Joanna closed her eyes again then and struggled to get back to it, to catch another glimpse of him.

But it was no use. The vision was gone. She opened her eyes again and rolled over on her back. *He's been dead nearly 30 years*, she thought. It was a winter night a lot like this. Cold, with the wind blowing and the snow drifting.

It was then that she became aware of sounds again, and she could hear that the gusting wind had not let up. She pushed the covers back, sat up on the edge of the mattress and then rose slowly to her feet, where she stood for a few seconds before taking those first few steps. At 75, getting out of bed took some care.

Joanna walked slowly through the living room of the large old house, into the dining room and peered out one of the big bay windows. In the darkness beyond, she searched for the dim outline of a telephone pole on the far side of the driveway. But she could see nothing but a blank wall of dark grey outside the window. She knew the blizzard was worse and dreaded the coming day if it didn't let up. She'd already spent one 24-hour stretch in the house, unable to get outside to feed her rabbits and the few cows she kept. The worst of it was that the phone had gone out.

Joanna turned away from the window and stared vacantly across the room, her hands clasped in front of her. She fought the welling loneliness, like she'd done countless times before. The feeling of being overwhelmingly alone had been Joanna's companion for 29 years. Yet she'd learned to endure solitude and to find pleasure in the very circumstances that isolated her.

After her husband, Will, died from a heart attack at the age of 50, Joanna faced the task of raising four children alone. She chose to do that by farming this farm where she and Will had worked since their wedding day. She loved the mystique of the animals and the personality of the land. Even now, as she turned back to the glass and watched fingers of snow scuttle into the corners of the window, she felt the will of the elements. In some uncanny sense, such awareness usually made her feel stronger, less alone—as if she were an integral part of some master scheme.

But tonight, the solitude—and another, less familiar, sadness enveloped her. She bit her lip to stop the tears, even though there were no children to be strong for. There was a time, she remembered, when this house rang with children's laughter.

Then suddenly, she wondered, why had it all come to an end?

The silver-haired woman slumped into a chair at the table and cried softly into her work-worn hands. There it was. She'd never faced the question so squarely, and it filled her with a grief she hadn't known since the day her husband died. Through all the years of work and worry she'd believed one day this land would provide a home and a living for a son or a daughter. She believed that grandchildren would explore the yard and fields where her children had roamed before, and that she would participate again in the family ceremonies of planning, struggling to meet goals—and dreaming. But she and Will must have failed. They hadn't left their children a legacy after all. Otherwise why was she here now alone?

From somewhere in the north wall of the house came an intermittent creaking, a rippling sound that signaled the strength of the battering gusts of wind.

Then, Joanna thought about the old photo album, the one that was filled with pictures of the kids when they were little. There would be a photo there of a cat Rachel used to dress in doll's clothes, of Bill fixing his motorcycle, and of Andrew pulling little Sarah in her wagon—and pictures of Will would be in that album, too.

She hurried to the glass-faced bookstand and searched through the encyclopedias, the Bible storybooks, the livestock care books and the various texts she'd acquired over the years.

She tried the office next. That room had been a creation of the last 20 years.

The futile search only added salt to her raw feelings. She went again to the window, to peer out into the darkness and to think. She left the window and went up the stairs, climbing slowly and carefully. At the top she turned down a short hallway. The room she entered at the end was filled with articles that spanned a lifetime and told the very history of the family: old books, old dolls, broken toy tractors, wood-framed prints and antique furniture. Joanna poked inside the various boxes, rummaging carefully through their contents. But the album was not there.

Slowly she walked back down the hall. The night seemed to stretch on forever before her.

Back at the stairs, instead of going down, she turned left into a room that had once belonged to her oldest son, Bill. After he'd left home, Andrew inherited it and, later on, Sarah. At the doorway, Joanna flipped on the light switch and surveyed the room. Its character had changed little since Bill's time. The bed was still pushed up against the east wall, the dresser against the south wall. Even the curtains were the same.

There was a box of books on the floor near the side of the bed. Sarah must have been looking through that box the last time she was home, Joanna thought. So many of her things were still there.

The woman stepped closer, and when she recognized the book at the very top of the box, tears filled her eyes. It was Will's old Bible, the one his brother had given to him on this 40th birthday, the one Joanna had later presented to Sarah as a keepsake. Gently she picked up the old book and began to leaf through it. Inside was a letter addressed to Sarah from a friend. There was a poem, too. Sarah had the habit of writing little poems or essays and leaving them in haphazard spots around the house.

Joanna read the poem slowly. Then, as she finished reading, she glanced from the scribbled words back at the Bible and happened to notice one more sheet of paper, folded in half and tucked inside the pages.

She set the poem aside and slipped the other piece of paper from its berth in the Bible and unfolded it. It was another of Sarah's writings, titled "To the Land, With Love." Joanna began to read:

"Whenever I return to visit this place of my growing up, I recognize again how indelibly it has stamped me. This farm is, at once, its own unique person and an integral part of my very being. Its demands, its rewards, its variety of faces—all have worked together to teach me about faith. To this day, the sight of the Big Dipper shining up in the northern sky transports me back to the well between the two barns.

"And I stand there again on a crisp winter night, waiting for a bucket to fill with water. As I stare up at those luminous stars, once more, belief pours over me. It is a belief, a faith, that life will follow its rightful course, and I will never forget the power of dreams.

"This farm is a place, too, where the south wind that blows on a March evening carries hope. Its balmy gusts are sated with excitement, with eagerness for the future to be unfurled. During those long evenings we spent choring in the darkness, I learned to listen closely for the messages borne on those winds. And their lessons stay with me, no matter where I am.

"It was the very land itself that taught me to accept aloneness, to be quiet—and to listen for the inner sounds that can only come from silence. It seems as though the soil itself has drawn in the sweat, the tears, and the endurance of the men who've plowed it.

"Some still days their presence is nearly palpable, and in my mind's eye I watch my father drive his John Deere up and down the furrows of the fields.

"By some divine alchemy the soil transforms what it has taken in and exudes . . . what? Love? Yes. I believe that's what I feel when I think of being there: love of God and love of all creation."

Joanna slowly folded the paper and slipped it back inside Will's Bible. She lifted the old leather-bound book and held it close for a moment.

Then, as she slowly reached to put it back in its resting place, she spied the worn cover of the photo album. Just underneath the Bible in the box. The sight made her feel like laughing, and as she opened it, she felt the same happiness she always felt when she opened the door of her home to a special friend.

She expected to see him. And sure enough, there was Will, dressed in his usual striped overalls, his hair windblown and his favored white cat cradled in his arms. He was smiling, almost smugly, as if he'd always known the thing that had eluded her for so long. She wasn't sure, then, if she spoke the words out loud, or if she only heard them in her heart: "Joanna. Why did you doubt? Didn't you know that you and I—and this land—we gave them everything!"

* * *

I wrote the short story in 1988. Only thinly disguised as fiction, the story was intended to be a tribute to my mother and her determination to raise her children on the farm. I scribbled the words out in longhand while sitting at a small, rickety table in the "night shack" of the Manitoba ranch where my husband, John, worked—and where I had worked for a number of years before our marriage. At the time I wrote the story I was serving as the night nursemaid to a bunch of cows that were calving in the cold of January. The second income from the night job supplemented the then-meager earnings I gleaned as an agricultural free-lance writer, work I did by day from a rented office in a town near the small farm John owned.

Stark inside and isolated as it was by the night, the little shack made a perfect writer's haven. The sentences that surfaced in between—and maybe because of—checking the cows every hour or half-hour, shined a spotlight on internal truths I had not found before.

When I stepped outside to check the cows, my breath hung about me in grey clouds before evaporating into the 30-degrees-below-zero night air. Steam rose, too, from the backs of the cows as they lay in their beds of deep straw in an open-fronted shelter. Yard lights illumined the corrals, but the shack sat in the darkness, beyond the rings of light.

Just as the cold gave form to my breath, the isolation and simplicity of the shack gave shape to insights about my youth spent on a family farm. The insights formed a spiritual chain linking the past to the present. I had suspected, when I began writing the short story, that the insights surfacing through the writing would illustrate the positive influence the family farm had had on my spirit. As I wrote the last words of the story, I saw my initial assumption to be true: The family farm had indeed served as a virtual classroom, teaching me much about faith, hope, and love; in effect, farm life had fitted me with a durable spiritual armor, equipping me with a tough resiliency to life.

This was an important revelation, since a number of years before I had found new meaning in the Apostle Paul's words: "So faith, hope, love abide, these three ... ." At the time, I was in my late-20s, single, buffeted by fear of the future and bouts of despondency. Struck by the meaning of the Apostle Paul's words, I reasoned that faith in God, hope, and love—all three working together in one's life—could serve as an armor to help one withstand and, indeed, live productively, through the uncertainties and adversities of life. Yet it was not until some seven years later, during my isolations in the night shack that a correlation dawned, and I began to see that my spirit had always had a good dose of faith, hope, and love—and that these strengths had been instilled in me, to a great extent, by my growing up on a farm.

The working out of the images, the thinking through of the concepts while writing the story was the proving ground for the positive outcome of my theory. Most importantly, I wanted the story to communicate to my mother how much I valued the spiritual gifts farm life had given me. And I wanted her to realize, too, the importance of the role she had played in this gifting process. In the years following my father's death in 1960, when I was six years old, my mother modeled faith and hope through her determination to keep trying, through her courage to keep moving forward. With myself and two older children yet to raise, she must have felt crushed by the weight of responsibility. Indeed, I see her yet, leaning into my Aunt Corinne's embrace as they stand in the doorway between the dining room and the hallway the night my father died . . . and I hear my mother's anguished question: "What am I going to do, Corinne?"

She might have supported us by teaching, but to do it, she would have had to return to college to keep pace with increasing educational standards for teachers. She chose the alternative, of continuing to farm without her husband. She chose hard work with her hands, seven days a week; she chose milking cows, carrying buckets of feed, scraping manure from milking platforms, washing equipment, and feeding dairy calves.

She chose prayer. I glimpse her still, through a narrow slit in the doorway to the bathroom, as she kneels by the bathtub to pray in privacy. Her choice demanded a quantum leap of faith into the unknown, a wilderness that brought us all seemingly insurmountable problems to overcome. But overcoming these taught each of us our own lessons about faith, hope, and perseverance.

Because my brother John, for example, became responsible for the farm work and the maintenance and repair of the tractors and general farm machinery at such a young age, his relative lack of experience due to his youth caused problems that could be particularly frustrating. Machinery is unforgiving. The only way to get through many of these problems was to innovate, and to simply have faith and hope that persistence would pay off. In recent letters he described to me how some of the frustrating incidents from his youth taught him the ability to face and embrace the hard things in life. One story he told took place when he was 15:

"In the spring of 1962, the first year that I was responsible for the field work, I had an incident that I have often considered my 'baptism by fire.' The incident served to galvanize my focus on getting things done without embarrassing myself in front of the community. I was plowing and seeding on Frank Eichorn's quarter south of us and was working my way closer and closer to the edge of the alkali gumbo spot on the southeast side of that big, low area that is now under water. I came too close and began to get stuck, so I unhooked the 720 tractor from the plow and moved it so I could pull the plow, packer, and drill out at an angle with a chain, which is what Dad had taught me to do.

"But I pulled at too much of an angle and tipped the plow over, with the plowshares pointing upward. This was clearly visible from the road, so I was starting to feel panicky and made a hasty decision to pull the plow the other way, without realizing it was too wet that direction. I sank the 720 to its belly and was stranded. At the time, we only had the old G for a second tractor, and I knew that was not going to help much. So I flagged down a neighbor and asked for help. ... I think the reason this incident was so traumatic for me was because the tractor and upside-down plow sat there all day, and many people driving by on the road slowed down to see what a mess I had made."

Another story he told was striking evidence of how we learned at a very young age to take responsibility for our actions:

"Dad had used an alcohol-based antifreeze in the tractors instead of the ethylene glycol we now use, which doesn't evaporate in hot weather. Dad was careful to make sure there was new antifreeze in the tractors each fall. Since that is what he did, I thought I should do the same. One year I somehow managed to forget that the alcohol in the tractors' antifreeze would evaporate over the summer—or else I just got caught by an early cold snap. At any rate, one morning I found icicles hanging from the 720 and discovered to my horror that the block of the cranking engine was cracked. After berating myself for being so stupid, I suddenly realized that the John Deere 70 diesel was built the same way. So I ran over to it and found that it, too, had a cracked starting-engine block. I fell to my knees and cried. I managed to rebuild both of those engines that fall and winter, but it was a very discouraging thing for me, mostly because of the cost and time I spent."

Hard lessons to be sure. But they kindled in us a tough persistence and ingenuity. These traits were forged stronger, I think, by our mother's unwavering belief in our abilities. Indeed, it could be that Mom's early belief in us shaped our attitudes and capabilities in ways we do not fully comprehend. A final story from my brother John illustrates our mother's trust:

"One very blustery and bitterly cold winter day, I went to get some hay from someone west of Kief. The roads were all blocked by normal standards, but I had adapted the truck for the snow by having only single tires on the back instead of dual tires. I put chains on the back tires, and then I loaded the truck with snow for weight and charged my way through huge snowdrifts, stopping to clean snow from the engine compartment periodically. When I reached my destination, I dumped the snow and loaded the hay. One of the neighbors saw me going by on the road and thought I was nuts to be out in such weather. The person called Mom to ask if she knew what her crazy son was up to. Mom simply told the caller that I knew what I was doing and could take care of myself."

My sister, Karen, too, learned as a teenager the responsibility of doing what had to be done, despite the awesomeness of the task. She discovered how to reach down inside herself and pull out the courage needed to do things she feared. I recall watching Karen's reaction after she treated a calf with a needle for the first time. I did not actually see her stick the needle into the calf's muscle . . . but I saw her afterwards, slouched against the manger in the horse stall, crying. I had not seen my sister cry before. Of the few memories I have from that time period, soon after my father's death, this is one of the more vivid. With inner eyes much older than my physical age of six or seven, I studied the meaning of this image: a young girl crying in the aftermath of doing a task that, moments before, had been too hard, a task for which the familiar hands of a father-teacher were absent.

Karen, in turn, must have been the one who taught me how to treat sick animals with a needle. For I do not recall how I learned; only that I learned. I suppose because I watched her and because she must have guided me through the first few times I treated an animal, I never experienced her emotional trauma.

But later on, when I was 19 or 20, I needed to treat a bloating cow, and I felt as Karen must have felt years before, crumpled against that horse manger. The incident of the bloated cow happened during the years when Mom and I tended the dairy herd alone:

One morning I discovered a cow whose stomach was badly bloated, causing her a great deal of pain and difficulty in breathing. Indeed, the cow was in danger of dying. I treated the cow with a drench, but the medicine didn't relieve the bloat. Then Mom and I threaded a hose down the cow's throat, hoping to drain some of the air off the cow's stomach, but we had no luck. In desperation I called the vet, describing the symptoms. Over the phone he told me how to give immediate relief to the cow: I was to insert a trocar into the animal's left side, letting some of the trapped air escape. But the incision had to be made in just the right spot, so as to avoid damaging vital tissues. Standing alone beside the cow in the chute, with my hand poised over her side, I second-guessed over and over my decisions about where to place the instrument. I felt too weak to stand, let alone plunge the knife-sharp trocar into the cow's side.

But I did it anyway.

Integral to the lessons farm life taught us about persistence, about learning the conviction to keep trying in spite of the fact that obstacles seemed insurmountable and in spite of the fact that we didn't know whether or not our efforts would yield "success," were the lessons, too, to persist by making use of the means at hand, which were frequently not the most ideal. Often we did not have the tools, experience, or resources needed to accomplish something. So we had to improvise the means and the methods.

Improvisation was a skill, or a knack, we learned from our farmer-parents, who were particularly adept at this, since they had lived through the Great Depression during the 1930s. A couple of old kitchen chairs John and I still have, chairs my mother and father used when they were first married in 1936, serve as testaments to my father's bent for improvisation. According to my mother's stories, they had no money to buy chairs so Dad rescued broken ones from his parents' junk heap. He fashioned wooden pieces for the missing parts, and braced the legs with wire twisted tight.

One chair was stripped of its curved, top crosspiece at the back. To replace this missing piece, Dad cut a small section from a wooden drill wheel taken from an old horse-drawn drill once used to seed fields to grain. He screwed the section from the wheel into the gaping hole in the back of the chair. The thickness of the wheel section suited the chair just right. In fact, few might have guessed the piece was improvised from a drill wheel if it hadn't been for the two spoke holes situated dead center in the piece. To fix these visual giveaways, Dad plugged them with a wood filler he concocted from glue and sawdust. When the fixing was finished, Mom varnished her "new" set of kitchen chairs and used them for a decade before getting others. The chair with the drill-wheel back sits in our basement yet, awaiting fresh paint. Still sturdy and serviceable, it's hard to imagine some 60 years have passed since the old thing was rescued from a junk heap.

Even after decades of being gone from the farm, my oldest brother, Forest, seemed to have never lost this knack for making something from nothing, this sense that all resources possess an innate value and that things appearing as "junk" for the moment hold intrinsic value because of the future needs they might fill. Forest's sense saved John a good deal of trouble not long ago, as the result of an incident when Forest and his family visited the farm the first summer John and I seeded a crop on the land.

A gear sprocket had broken on the old Van Brunt seed drill John was using that summer. The drill was one Forest had also used when he helped my father with the field work as a youth and when he farmed the land for a short time after Dad's death. Working together, Forest and John loosened a shaft and removed the bracket for a slow-down gear, which allowed the drill shaft to rotate more slowly, so that very fine seed, such as millet seed, could be seeded accurately. John was about to toss the gear in the garbage, when Forest said, "You're not going to throw that away, are you?" His remark caused John to change his mind and hang the part on the wall in the shop.

Eleven years later, John wanted to use a different drill to seed millet, but found that the drill was missing its slow-down gear. The gear hanging in the shop fit the newer drill perfectly.

A PRAYER FOR THE PRAIRIE

* * *

And so it has been down through the generations of people reared on family farms: Unpredictable and often daunting circumstances have shaped our faith and hope, forged our determination, and honed our inventiveness. Mother Nature, too, has kneaded the people of the land like clay in her hands, baking and chiseling those who will yield, into resilient, pliable creatures who can endure life's adversity and turbulence . . . like the sturdy gumweed that survives overgrazing and like the salt grass thriving in soil where other plants perish. Because of that, I think, the family-farm and family-ranch culture is a repository of hope and faith. It is a culture containing a remnant of people who understand that life's seasons of joy and pain, ease and hardship, success and failure come as surely to mankind as do the seasons of summer and winter. Indeed, my most treasured spiritual gifts from the farm are the lessons I have learned during the times of hardship and adversity.

"Of all the lessons the life and the land taught me, I value most their teachings about faith and hope," I said in an essay written more than a decade ago. "I learned to lean on the trust that even the most bitter, death-like winter would dissolve into life-giving spring. I knew that for every chore rendered nearly unbearable by a brutal blizzard or an impossible knee-deep blanket of wet snow, there would be chores softened by the balmy breezes of a summer evening. Work would turn to play on days filled with the sweet scent of prairie roses and the peaceful cooing of the mourning doves in the elms.

"Maybe it's those very seasonal extremes for which North Dakota is famous that produce so much tenacity in its children. For once you have internalized the conviction that spring always follows even the cruelest of winters, then—through some alchemy in the soul—that belief overshadows the events of your days. As a result, disappointments are seldom seen as devastating roadblocks. They become, instead, simply open doors to another direction. Farm and ranch life is fraught with opportunities to learn such faith—to believe that most problems can be solved, the rest can be endured, and new opportunities will always appear.

"I remember one incident from my childhood that provided me with a particularly good chance to learn to look ahead to a new direction and not stare behind me at the disappointment. The long-awaited day when our purebred Arab mare broke her standing habit of foaling only male foals had finally arrived. True to my dreams, the mare gave us a filly. But she had a difficult delivery, and the filly died.

"I was heartbroken. I'd counted on the filly's coming for a long time. Then, that evening, offering me the simple but powerful comfort that brought light to her own dark hours, my mother said, 'Tomorrow is a new day.' So I went to bed, trying hard to believe that the dawn would indeed—somehow—bring some salve for this hurt. And it did. When morning came, I resolutely turned my thoughts to the other colts the spring would bring.

"Like all farmers, my mother kept her face turned toward that new day. Rain was sure to come—if not this year, then next. The crop may be a failure now, but next year's was sure to be better. And while that hope was not always expressed in words, it was evident in her determined step, in her plans for next year, and in her persistent attack on the weighty work load she bore.

"From such tilth are born faith and hope. And in the years that have passed ... I've realized how vital these traits are for productive living. For life is full of bitter winters, crop failures, and those special colts that slip away. My days on that farm taught me that, as surely as there are difficulties, just as surely are there new directions and new opportunities. No winter ever comes that isn't an open door toward some spring."

WHERE TWO OR THREE
ARE GATHERED

2002

One morning, before settling down to work, I visited my mother in her bedroom. It was during the time when John and I shared the farmhouse with her. My mother, who was 89, sat in her green chair by the old triple windows lining the east wall of the room. Her silver-white hair shone in the sunlight streaming over her shoulders. As she leafed through the pages of her Bible, she barely lifted her eyes to acknowledge my presence. She searched the pages with the same intensity with which she once searched the dictionary for a word. A teacher at heart, my mother had always loved reading and the gathering of ideas.

"What are you looking for?" I asked.

"Last night I dreamed of a beautiful verse in the Bible, but now I can't remember its words," she said. "I was hoping I could find it." Despite not being able to recall the specific words she had dreamed, my mother indeed remembered the sense of grace the words bequeathed. They spoke to her of the shortfalls of her life, she said. But the message was surely borne on wings of love, because her manner was almost giddy as she told me of her dream.

The words of the verse, she said, had come in a radiance spilling down from the sky, filling the back yard with light.

Listening to my mother's story, I felt weight lift from my shoulders. I sensed God's grace had indeed visited my mother in the night, and I hoped she would draw long-lasting comfort and courage from the memory. As the years of old age had robbed my mother of independence and capabilities, her faith seemed to flounder. "What good am I?" she would demand some days while we drank our afternoon coffee. I sensed the depth of her discouragement, and her question always caused me to wrack my brains for ways to encourage her. I may have wrongly tried to take over God's work, but I felt responsible—as did my siblings—for my mother's faith. When faith left her, I believed there should be ways by which I could serve as a catalyst for its return.

To encourage her, I urged my mother to pray and to appreciate the power in prayer. "Look at all the people who need prayers, all the people who need God's help," I said. "These days could be the most important of your life because of the free time you have now to pray."

"But why should God listen to me?" she would often counter.

Indeed, why should God listen?

This frequent reply of hers tried my own faith and energy. I myself felt abandoned in a wilderness; I felt that a great chasm had opened between God and me, spanning a distance that swallowed my prayers in an abyss. Following her retort, I would sit in silence, filled with a heavy tiredness. Mentally, I tried to cast such moments to God, faith or no faith. Yet I still felt the weight of the stone that was the responsibility for my mother's faith and her peace of mind—or lack of it. I yearned for a spiritual certainty to fill my mother with peace and trust during the years of her old age.

But the dream my mother had had of misty light spilling down from heaven lifted my burden, because for a time, the memory of the dream seemed to rekindle my mother's hope and enthusiasm. She struggled again to overcome her own fears, focusing outside herself as much as she could.

Her efforts to overcome marked even the last day she lived on her farm, the last time we sat together in her yard. It was a day in June only a short time after my mother's dream, and the irises north of the house still bloomed. I had set my mother's lawn chair beside the flowers, so she could sit in the sun near them whenever she chose. It was late in the afternoon and I was working in my upstairs office when I saw my mother through the window. She leaned heavily on her cane, walking slowly, step by measured step across the yard to sit in her chair by the flowers.

I went back to my work of trying to assimilate the information for the technical article I was writing. The article discussed the cattle disease anaplasmosis, its symptoms, how the disease spreads, and ways livestock producers could reduce its spread. It was too late in the day to be working on such a technical, information-laden project. Indeed, I was beginning to feel so weary I could barely think. Looking up from my desk, I watched my mother through the window. She seemed so small and alone, sitting by the flowers, looking straight ahead. Since my thoughts about anaplasmosis had simply stopped, I decided I would accomplish more by sitting outdoors beside my mother, even if I didn't have the energy to visit with her.

Outside, I ease down beside her on a deep log slab John cut from a dead cottonwood and placed by the irises, to encourage passersby to rest by the flowers. Mom and I sit beside each other in silence for a bit. "It's really nice out this afternoon," I say finally. Turning toward me, my mother nods.

"You look pale," she says. "Do you feel all right?"

"I'm just tired."

"What are you writing?" she asks, squinting more than usual, even though we sit facing north, looking away from the sun. "Are you writing anything interesting?"

I bristle inside, but I know what she means. For 15 years I've written mostly about technical agricultural topics, telling information-based stories about what other people are doing. Like many writers, my early aspirations centered on churning out poetry, novels, essays. Yet my bread-and-butter work is worlds away from such writing. I'm thankful for the experience, insights, and training that have come with my work.

It's the fulfillment of an early dream, the answer to countless prayers. But lately, I've been chafing at the bit, starting to notice the confinement of technicality, yearning for time to write more free-roaming words, words drawing from my personal experience.

I tell my mother what I'm writing about, but she doesn't seem to understand; she doesn't respond. Then I add, passing my hand across my face: "I sure look forward to doing more personal writing."

My mother senses my deep yearning, and her old-time habit of encouraging others rises up past her faltering faith for herself and her own future. Though the light in her eyes seems oddly flat, her voice is strong and adamant. "Oh, yes!" Then thumping her chest, she adds, "People like to read I, I, I, I . . . I."

And though she has long stopped reading the articles I bring her occasionally—the pieces I've written that have parts I think might interest her—she adds a line of further encouragement that she has told me always; it never varies: "What I like so well about your writing is how your words flow together!" As she speaks, she sweeps her arm through the air in front of her, squinting, the light in her eyes perplexingly flat. Regardless of whether her words are true or false, they serve their purpose. A spark of hope rekindles my perseverance, and in a few minutes I go back to work, telling myself one day I will write of matters springing from my spirit.

In early evening my mother suffers a stroke. An ambulance takes her away, and she does not return to the farm.

The stroke paralyzed my mother's right side. She recovered from it well enough in a period of weeks to be able to speak again, to eat with assistance, and to sit upright in a wheelchair. But her needs were too great for us to continue caring for her at home. My sister Karen, my brother John, and I admitted her to a care center 20 miles from the farm. The stroke stripped away nearly all of my mother's remaining independence and self-sufficiency, banishing her from her home, her trees, her birds, and the distant hills. My own sense of God's abandonment increased.

My visits to my mother now seem surreal. In the afternoons I seek her familiar head in a room filled with heads of silver-grey. I find her: She sits in her wheelchair, unaware that I am watching and oddly askew from a cluster of other elders in wheelchairs. She speaks to the nearest with determined brightness, trying to draw the other into conversation, forcing her words past a sagging jaw, new in its awkwardness. Yet her resolute advance draws no response.

Other days I find her by a glass bird cage, studying the inmates as she once studied the swallows building nests on the porch at home, the swallows who scolded us as we drank our afternoon coffee together.

At night, I toss and turn in my own bed, finding it hard to breathe, seeing my mother, trapped.

My mother . . . she once soared like a hawk, high overhead, alone in the sky, careening on the currents of a gusting prairie wind. Now, her wings hang limp and motionless, brushing the floor of a cage. I am trapped there beside her.

Some afternoons I wheel her outside so we can sit in the sun and set our faces to the breeze from the west. Once, she asked, "Am I ever going to go home again, or am I just going to die here?"

I fix my eyes on her face in silence. My mind will not shape an answer.

There are other days, days when my mother's fragility evokes from her an uncharacteristic vulnerability. Turned inside out, it becomes strong. It is the vulnerability in her smile and the light in her eyes when she sees me coming across the room. It is the brush of her left hand on my cheek when I kneel by her wheelchair. And it is in a memory from the past, rising one day seemingly unbidden, like a deer startled from its bed in the buckbrush:

"When Roy died, I lost all my faith," she said abruptly during one of my visits. "When he died, it was like a fragile chord from heaven to earth had been cut."

Yet on this day, in the lee of the memory of old pain, faith is reborn, and my mother's fears subside. "I'm just going to trust God," she says. "He knows what's best for me."

Some weeks pass. It is another visit to my mother in the care center. After coming indoors from our sit in the sun, she asks to be wheeled to her room. There, I read to her from the 37th Psalm: "Commit your way to the Lord; trust in him, and he will act. ... Be still before the Lord, and wait patiently for him; ... The steps of a man are from the Lord, and he establishes him in whose way he delights; though he fall, he shall not be cast headlong, for the Lord is the stay of his hand."

The words seem as much for me as for my mother.

It is time to go. I hug her and kiss her face. As I walk toward the door, Mom tells me she likes the new resident who moved in down the hall.

When I come again, it is with my husband John, my sister Karen, and my niece Stephanie. My mother lies motionless on the narrow bed, her face peaceful and immobile. She is not there. She is soaring again, high overhead, wings outspread in the graceful, spiraling slow-dance of a hawk aloft on a gentle prairie breeze.

I know that God hears her prayers.

More than two years have passed since my mother's death. I have returned again and again to the 37th Psalm, to find her reborn presence there. I sense her spirit has passed through a screen of healing, healing available to each of us. As time passes, the surety of the healing strengthens . . . and I am amazed. The stone has been lifted from my shoulders. After a long silence, God has answered with healing, the years of a prayer-gathering of one woman's family.

A PRAYER FOR THE PRAIRIE

My mother's joyful dream of light filling the back yard seems, in retrospect, a milestone, a turning point, God's reassurance that His hand was indeed at work in the healing of my mother's spirit; so often storm-tossed by troubles and cares from the past. When I relive the memory of her telling me the story of her dream, I am amazed at how her vision unfolded in a setting to which many people have invested their faith, hope, and love, expressing these gifts through the labor of their hands and the vision of their imaginations.

Behind the house an unusual stone marked by a natural cross testifies to these investments, small yet not-so-small sacrifices of self for another, sacrifices spanning the generations yet building upon each other. The unusual stone rests on the ground on the east side of the house. It sits beside one of two tall spruce trees my mother planted soon after she and my father bought the farm in 1946. Fifty years ago my father found the stone in a field and placed it behind the house, facing the open-fronted porch. The grey stone, deep and oblong, is ribbed with two intersecting rings of material resembling limestone. The ribs jutting from the surface form the shape of a cross.

I do not know my father's intentions when he set the stone in place. But I have always considered it to be a perennial benediction for his family and home; his wrestling of the rock from the earth and his tugging and pulling of it into place behind his home, his personal prayer as enduring as the stone.

It would seem he brought the great rock to the back yard because he envisioned this to be a special place, a focal point for his family. Yet for long years after his death during my childhood, the back yard and the spacious porch behind the house were, for the most part, abandoned. Grass overgrew Mom's flower garden near the stone, and the lilac bushes growing at the base of the porch loomed thick and entwining, eventually blocking any entrance or view from the porch to the yard. We hardly ever spent time in the back yard except to mow grass.

But as my brother John matured, as the time neared when he would make a life for his own away from the farm, it seems, as I look back, that he began to imagine conditions on the farm as they should be ideally, conditions it would need to carry it forward into the future in his absence. For a period of years he seemed consumed by an almost frenetic drive to accomplish things; to rush to get to the end of a long list of tasks he needed to finish before he could set out on a life of his own. I think he was building a nest for my mother and me, securing a future for the farm, providing a way for us to live and work there despite the absence of the oldest children. In those years he never walked but ran from point to point. I caught his habit, finding exhilaration in the pace.

Designing and building the labor-reducing milking parlor was his priority. The parlor would secure the farm's income because it would let Mom and me milk more cows and yet be able to handle the workload. But building fences and planting new tree shelterbelts were on his list, also, as was the partial renovation of the house and the back porch. He tore out the obscuring lilac bushes, returning a view to the porch. He created a walkway along the south side of the house and a concrete landing for the porch, constructing new steps and installing new side railing and supports for the porch. In this way he worked out his vision for greater life for the back yard.

All the while, Dad's stone cross looked on.

Then, the time came for my brother to leave. And he did. Yet much of him stayed. He returned for a part of each summer to put up hay, and he remained poised to come back to help in emergencies.

Still, the porch and the back yard went unused, its spacious, simple beauty largely unappreciated. Years passed, as Mom and I pressed our noses to the labor of tending cattle and running a dairy. My sister, Karen, returned to the farm to help with the work. Then she married Arlo and moved to their farm nearby. In time, I left, too, and though I returned often, and though Karen and Arlo helped her frequently, our mother worked mostly alone, continuing to milk and feed her cows. The grass in the back yard sometimes grew tall, resembling a hayfield more than a yard. Once, while my brother Forest and his wife, Grace, were visiting Mom, Forest and I cut the tall yard grass with a small, sickle mower, pitching the grass into piles, which we hauled away with a pickup.

Then I returned to the farm for good, with my husband, John. John brought visions of a back yard beauty he had known from his childhood lived in a yard where roses bloomed and white and pink peonies burst from dense shrubs in spring; where children tumbled, laughing, in short, green grass; and where a mother played croquet with as much exuberance as her children. He set his hands to work at once, pruning the dying apple tree, hauling years' worth of tin cans from the old ash pile north of the house, and dragging to a more isolated spot the machinery parked to the east of the house, in full view of the back porch.

At first my mother could only see his work as an invasion of her territory, a threat to her control. These feelings seemed to last a long time. But my husband persevered, continuing to beautify her yard despite the fact that we had a farmyard and a home of our own 10 miles away to tend as well. John stood firm in his belief that the beauty and tranquility of the back yard would gradually infiltrate my mother's spirit, bringing her a greater measure of joy and peace. So he continued to work, bearing her demonstrations of disapproval.

The stone cross looked on.

And My John placed a smaller stone beneath it, to lift the cross, bringing it into sharper focus to a bystander on the porch.

In time, my mother began to get her own ideas about beautifying the yard. She and my brother John's wife, Mary, planted irises, a peony, and tiger lilies in the earth my husband had hauled in to cover the hole where the old ash pile had been. And Mom ordered fruit trees, along with a maple and weeping willows—and over the years numerous other trees of which many died—that John and I helped her to plant back of the house where the old machinery had been. Then My John and I added a log flower bed in one corner of the yard.

The years passed, and the trees and flowers grew. My mother became weaker, and My John and I moved in to share the farmhouse with her, caring for her in the warm-weather months of the year. Some weekends she spent with Karen and Arlo. During the winter and early spring she lived in Spokane with my brother John and Mary, and their daughters. As my mother's strength lessened, she spent hours in the summer sitting at the picnic table My John placed on the back porch. She watched the birds and simply drank in the view, which had indeed taken on the luminescent beauty that it now expresses in summer.

The maple tree growing behind the old twin spruces sways gracefully in the breeze, already reaching some 15 feet toward the sky. Behind it stands a graceful young weeping willow. Three rows of fruit trees and shrubs run north and south. The trees yield apples, cherries, and apricots. Karen and I picked the apricots and several gallons of the cherries one summer, and from the fruit Karen made a colorful, tart sauce. In fall the boughs of the old apple tree My John healed through pruning droop to the ground, laden with reddish-green apples that we store in boxes, giving us fruit throughout the winter.

On clear mornings in early summer the sunlight filters through the tops of the old cottonwoods marking the east boundary of the back yard. The waxy leaves of the trees reflect the light, glimmering like emeralds. The filtered light causes a handful of half-grown Russian olive trees growing behind the old apple tree to appear as feather plumes of greyish green. In full bloom, the peony north of the porch adds an accent of fuchsia to the yard's color scheme.

Mom's bedroom and private living room offered direct access to the porch. The more time she spent there in summer, the more she came to appreciate the work of my husband, who continued to prune the trees and trim the grass of the large yard. He often mowed, too, a long angle through the cottonwoods to the northeast—an invitation to the eye to take in the distant view through a natural opening in the trees. "You should see how my son-in-law keeps the yard," she would sometimes say to people at church or some other social event. With a dramatic sweep of her arm, she would add, "It looks just like a park!"

Mom loved to walk with someone through her back yard. Such walks became nearly a ritual of my sister Karen's visits to my mother on warm summer days. After drinking coffee on the back porch, Mom would lead Karen around the yard, showing her the progress of the apricot trees, the fruit setting on the Nanking cherry bushes, and the weeping willow she considered to be a memorial to her husband. Mom walked slowly, her left hand firmly gripping Karen's and her right hand on her cane.

When my brother John and his wife, Mary, came with their daughters, Kresha and Katie, for summer visits to the farm, the back porch buzzed with life, especially during back yard picnics. Karen and her husband, Arlo, and their daughter, Stephanie, would join us, and My John would barbecue chicken.

The year the farm had been in my father's and my mother's ownership for 50 years, we hosted a family celebration. My brother Forest's daughters, Wanda and Donna, came. With Donna came her husband, Steve, and their three children—Heather, Lauren, and Jonathan. My mother sat on the back porch listening to her granddaughters' laughter and watching her great-granchildren play in the back yard. Some consolation, maybe, for the absence of her eldest son Forest, who, like his father, died before his time.

Like an observant but retiring patriarch standing at the center of the family's activity and yet often unseen, the stone cross looked on.

It is a cold morning in early March. John and I have just finished hauling three hayracks of millet to the cows and part of a rackful of alfalfa to the heifers. I guard the open gate to the heifer pen as John drives Pete and Skeet through it. Sparrows sing from the bushes and trees bounding the north and south sides of the pen. Though they are winter birds, their music reminds me that spring cannot be far off.

After the horses and the rack pass through the gate, I close it and cross the back yard, covered now with a crusted blanket of snow. On this day, the yard is silent and empty. But life will bloom here again in spring. It is true, John and I have no children, but the beauty of this place will not go unappreciated. It will be shared with others. John's extended family is large, and we expect his brothers and sisters and nieces and nephews to visit, as many already have. My family will return from time to time, and friends will join us here for meals or coffee. More importantly, the back yard is where John and I re-energize ourselves. Nearly every warm-weather day, we rest for a few minutes here, sitting on the porch or on lawnchairs beside the twin spruces. Some days the breeze and the bird songs calm my frustrations; on other days the distant view and the murmuring of the leaves of the cottonwoods restore my hope and my vision of the future.

On this cold morning in March I walk to the sunny side of the spruces, to the big grey stone my father wrestled into place before I was born. I lean down and brush the snow from its surface, exposing the cross. I wish I had known my father. I have only faint glimpses of him in my memory, a vague sense of a whisker-rough cheek rubbing mine. I wonder what he would think of our horse-partners and the significance of our work. I wonder what he would think if he could see the steel Noxall evener my husband uses to hitch Pete and Skeet to the hayrack onto which we load hay by hand. It is his evener, the one with which he hitched his team of blonde Belgians to the stoneboat and drove them to the hay meadow northeast of the yard the night that he died.

I wonder what my father's thoughts were the day he wrestled this stone into place. He was a quiet man of prayer, who loved the words of the Bible and particularly those of the 100th Psalm: "Know that the Lord is God! It is he that made us, and we are his; we are his people, and the sheep of his pasture. ... For the Lord is good; his steadfast love endures for ever, and his faithfulness to all generations." Knowing this, it is hard for me to imagine that my father did not consciously pray at some point in the process of positioning the stone cross behind his house.

Whatever the prayer, I believe it still echoes across the decades. It joined with his family's prayers when we prayed for my mother. My father's prayers joined, too, with those of my mother . . . for I know she prayed, despite the days when she felt God's deafness. Only months before her death she blessed the meal at a family gathering. She prayed while seated at the head of the big oak table, flanked by grandchildren and great-grandchildren. I remember being amazed. Despite growing inconsistencies in her everyday speech due to age, my mother's speaking voice while praying regained its old-time clarity and fairly rang clear to heaven, eloquent in timbre and turn of phrase, earnest in humility and thankfulness. In my memory, her prayer calls out as coming from one whose spirit resembles that of a prophet wandering in the wilderness. Indeed . . . maybe that's what she was.

My parents' prayers formed a legacy of prayer that has spread to their children and their families. It is a legacy, too, of forgiveness, a tradition of laying down pieces of ourselves for each other. Without it, I wonder, would I be standing here beside this stone cross in the first place? Would so many of my own demons have fled? Would My John and I do the work we do now? Would this family farm remain?

On this day I feel anchored by this heritage of prayer, engulfed in a Strength from outside myself. For the God who sometimes seems distant is also the Father of the Son who said: " ... if two of you agree on earth about anything they ask, it will be done for them by my Father in heaven. For where two or three are gathered in my name, there am I in the midst of them."

WHERE
PRAIRIE ROSES GROW
2002

It is nearly noon as John guides Pete and Skeet down the
wagon trail heading northwest of the yard. The temperature is
10 degrees above zero with a stiff north wind blowing. We're getting our
third and final load of millet hay to feed to the cows. After we pitch this
last load off back at the farmyard, I'll go to the house to fix a hot lunch
while John unhooks Pete and Skeet from the wagon and feeds them
alfalfa hay. They'll rest in the barn until late in the afternoon, when we'll
go after a couple of loads of wild hay from three-quarters of a mile south
of the farm.

On this last trip for the morning, as the horses and the wagon retrace
their tracks in the snow leading back to the millet field, a flock of horned
larks flits ahead. They have been feeding along the trail on the millet
seeds that have shaken off the hay we've hauled. The larks, winter
residents of our open fields, seem impervious to the cold and the wind,
which I find uncomfortable. Even with the thick felt hood shielding my
face, the wind stings. John turns his face to the side, too, in order to bear
the brunt of the north wind.

When we get to the stack, he parks the rack on the south side of the
big mound of hay, with Pete and Skeet facing west. He dallies the lines
around an upright brace at the front of the rack and then steps down to
unhook each horse's inside trace from the singletrees at their hocks. The
singletrees are fastened to the evener attached to the wagon. John
unhooks the inside trace for safety's sake. If, for some reason, the team

were to spook ahead while we were loading hay, they would have to bear the full weight of the pull on their bridle bits. This doesn't guarantee they won't spook, but it will probably prevent them from dragging the wagon far.

The millet hay is light to pitch, so the wind sometimes carries forkfuls of it beyond the rack. We try to fork with precision. To avoid the biting wind, I work with my back to it, feeling encumbered by the felt hood and my thick winter suit. I hardly notice that John has stopped working and has taken off his glove to pick up something up from the hay.

"Here, Ann," he says, using my middle name.

In his bare hand is the dried, feathered head of a crossbred millet plant. The seeds cascade from the stem in clusters, colored in pastel tones of yellow, green, purple, and pink. With the winter wind blowing at our backs, he presents the millet head and its long stem as he presents the flowers he brings home from the fields or the pastures in summer. Before the grass turns completely green in spring, he brings me dandelions and sets them in a small glass of water on the kitchen table. Later, in midsummer, he brings me sprigs of scarlet mallow, a low-growing plant with a sweet-scented flower of apricot-colored petals. Scarlet mallows grow near the meadow where my father died.

Searching through my clothing, I look for a place to safekeep the millet head for the trek home. Finding no such place, I stick the stem into a crack in the wooden crosspiece at the front of the hayrack. But John picks it from there, opens his coat, and tucks the millet stem into a long, narrow pocket at the top of his Carhartt winter overalls, where it will be safe till we get home.

We return to pitching hay onto the rack, and several more unusually colored heads of crossbred millet plants turn up, along with a few bright-red rose hips, the round fruit of the prairie rose. Prairie roses grow like weeds here on the old Eighty, springing up despite cultivation. They seem to thrive in areas where growing conditions are more difficult, such as here on the Eighty, where the soil is not particularly rich and tends to lose its moisture quickly.

Prairie roses spring up along roadsides, too. In early summer pink blooms pepper the side of the gravel road leading from the farm to Kief. From the edge of the dusty, dry roadbed the thorny little plants push fragile blossoms toward the sun. In a few days the petals fade and drop to the ground, and the round ball of a rose hip begins to form in the flower's place. After a killing frost in fall, rose hips turn bright red and begin to harden. The fruit has orangish flesh, with a cluster of tough seeds at the center. The red balls cling to the stems throughout fall and winter.

I keep a jar of dried, ground rose hips in our fridge. When we feel a cold or flu coming on but have no echinacea leaves, I make a tea from ground rose hips, ginger, and dried alfalfa leaves. The rose hips in our fridge are always a gift from my sister, Karen. She has perfected the discipline and processes needed to gather and store wild plants, in spite of her busy days as a mother and a partner in the farm and business she and Arlo own. Karen picks the rose hips after a hard frost, dries them on screens in the sun or upstairs in their house. After the hips dry, she grinds them and put them in the freezer.

Our house cat, Jeb, loves to see "Aunt" Karen come for visits. Often—especially on Christmas Eve—she brings him little cloth packets stuffed with catnip, which she has picked in the summer and dried. Jeb licks and bites the catnip toys until they're soggy and then bats them across the floor of the living room.

Besides picking dandelion and sow thistle greens in summer for salads, Karen also harvests (with gloves on) the tender tips of stinging nettle to steam and serve as a vegetable with a meal. In early spring she serves raw the tender, young shoots of cattails growing on the edge of a slough. In fall she picks buffalo berries and chokecherries to add to her "spitty-pitty" fruit soup made from Nanking bush cherries, thorn apples, plums, and Juneberries. One fall she grew barley in a window sill, which she dried and ground for barley green. Before winter set in that year, she potted the chicory plants from her garden, and gave us a couple of the pots. I set them in the house in the sunlight and harvested the greens for fresh salads throughout the winter.

Karen and I go for walks together only rarely, but when we do, the walk is filled with the wonder of discovery, for Karen has an explorer's spirit. We examine odd-shaped piles of stones on pasture hills: Is someone buried here? We study the damage a beaver has done to trees along a wetland: Is the beaver an invader here or a native of this landscape? If the beaver is a native, why does there not seem to be a natural process in place to heal its damage?

Karen's ability to find wonder in the commonplace influenced me when I was a child. Because of her, I learned at an early age the beauty and miraculousness of the birthing process, for instance. I was 10 years old when my heifer, Taffy, was about to calve. I came with Karen to the barn to see whether or not the calf had been born yet. When I peered into the pen, I saw my heifer lying on her side with a slimy, brown body protruding partway from her hindquarters. I gasped and turned to flee.

"No, it's all right," Karen said calmly. "Come back. Taffy is all right. This is wonderful to watch." I tiptoed back to the pen and peeked, amazed, through the boards of the gate. Taffy's sides heaved, pushing the slimy brown body farther outside of herself. Then, with a final heave and gush of fluid, Taffy's calf was born, flopping its forequarters and shaking its wet head. Every spring since, I've looked forward to calves being born.

Goethe has written, "A man should hear a little music, read a little poetry, and see a fine picture every day of his life in order that worldly cares may not obliterate the sense of the beautiful which God has implanted in the human soul." Living life on the land supplies such beauties. Every day brings me music, poetry, and fine art when I open my inner eyes and let myself be amazed, when I take the time and care to see the uncommon in the commonplace; to listen for the extraordinary in the ordinary.

My husband isn't the only one showing me beauty on this cold, windy day. Skeet offers a gift, too: It is John's ritual that, after we finish loading the hay and before he rehooks the inner traces for the trek home, he walks around to the front of the horses, checking bridles and collars, looking for any piece of harness that could be out of place. After we had finished pitching on the second load, I noticed that when John passed around to the front of Skeet, the stoic horse—who, unlike Pete, tends to express little affection—looked straight ahead as John passed in front of him, but flopped his lower lip a couple of times. But when I passed in front, though I reached out, as John commonly does, to stroke his face, his lower lip was still. After the third load is pitched on, I watch closely as John performs his ritual of inspection, and see that Skeet again flips his lower lip as John passes in front of him. The subtle affection gives me fascinating new insight into Skeet's character. Of the two horses, I had thought Pete was most attached to my husband. Now I'm not so sure.

Because of my constant presence in their workdays, Pete and Skeet have grown more used to me, and I've become less intimidated by them. More and more, I see myself driving them; I can feel the weight of the reins in my hands. Over the course of the winter, as I've sat near John at the front of the rack, I've seen how he handles Pete's occasional outbursts of fear, times when Pete—the son of a mare who had a career as a rodeo bronc—bunches his body and lunges forward into the bridle.

The worst episode happened earlier in the winter. We had fed one load of hay to the cattle and were approaching the feeding area with our second load. During our absence, a flock of wild turkeys had arrived, and were walking across the feeding area as we neared. From a distance, the flock looked like small army of Martians trudging across the field. Pete could hardly contain his fear, see-sawing back and forth in the harness, threatening to bolt. Even Skeet got nervous. John stopped the team and let them simply look at the birds for a while. Then he eased up on the lines ever so slightly, giving the big horses the freedom to move forward slowly and cautiously. They eventually relaxed, but not until after the turkeys had crossed over into the alfalfa field.

It is a warmer day in March when I drive Pete and Skeet. The temperature is 40 degrees above and a gentle southern breeze has blown all day, melting nearly all of the snow. John and the team have hauled round bales of hay from a neighbor's meadow for a good part of the day, so the horses have already put on about 14 miles by the time we head out to the alfalfa field with the hayrack to pick up feed for the heifers. We are at the west base of the Prayer Hill, when John asks, "Do you want to drive?"

I do and so he stops the team; I slide onto the bench seat and pick up the reins. "Step!" I command, and the big grey-white horses step ahead. We jog a bit along the trail leading through the alfalfa. "Eeeasy," I singsong, pulling back on the lines. The horses slow to a walk, we swing wide to the right, and then I pull heavier on the left line, and the horses fan gradually to the left, and then ahead, pulling the rack alongside a stack of alfalfa. I say "whoa," and the horses stop. I drove them once before, and when I said "whoa," they jumped ahead a bit, startled at my unfamiliar voice of authority. They are used to hearing me speak only in conversational tones.

After we finish pitching on a load of alfalfa for the heifers, I walk around to the front of the team and stroke Skeet's forehead. He lifts his nose and lets me press it against my face. Pete has shown this affection to me before but not Skeet. The big-man horses are growing accustomed to a woman's touch.

I drive the team and wagonload of hay toward home, and we pass again along the slope of my Prayer Hill. Life has changed much since I made my daily pilgrimages to its summit, weighed down by deep discouragement, fearing that the difficulties of farming were finally going to force us to leave. I feel more peaceful now; I sense God's purposes enveloping me like a warm blanket.

The very fact that I sit here on this hard wagon bench, holding the lines to a team seems the evolution of a purpose, one that I had not ever envisioned. It has been John's vision that this should happen. It has been his long-held hope that—as much as is possible—we could transition the farm's power source away from fuel-burning machines, to horses. He has long envisioned a haying process of harvesting and feeding loose hay— as opposed to baled hay—with horses and pitchforks. For many years I resisted. I was afraid we would get the hay put up only to find that it was impossible to feed in winter. The wind blows so often here; all I could see was light, loose hay blowing away in the wind when we tried to pitch it by hand. But pitching hay this winter has shown me that there are ways to work around the wind, especially if we keep a partial supply of bales on hand to feed to the livestock on days when wind prevents pitching.

There's no doubt the experiment has paid off financially. It's been nearly six months since John started a tractor. For the entire winter we have spent no money on fuel, oil, or repairs, even though we've fed some 75 head of cattle and a small remuda of saddle horses along with the work team.

Indeed, the very fact that we have cattle to feed at all is an answer to prayer and the fleshing in of a long-held vision. On the top of my dresser is a "cowboy" poem John wrote for me as a Christmas gift in 1992, two years after we moved to North Dakota from John's small farm in Manitoba:

> *This life of ranchin' and farmin' might make us go 'break,'*
> *But that feelin' soon leaves us with every long hike we take.*
>
> *From Ma Nature we've learned to return more than we take;*
> *This bizness of HRMing* sure ain't no fake.*
>
> *We've both faced this life with big hearts and no fear;*
> *And I've got a feelin' the neatest part is near.*

This feelin's real sharp, and its message quite clear;
So I'm wishin' you a Healthy and also a Happy New Year.
(*HRM stands for Holistic Resource Management.)

Though he officially owned no cattle at the time, John signed the Christmas card with his brand, a running JN, a brand he had never used and which had not then yet been registered with the North Dakota Stockmen's Association. Before our move to North Dakota, John sold the small herd of cattle he owned in Manitoba. Afterward, between buying farm equipment, paying cash rent to my mother for the farmland, and making a downpayment on the small farmstead we bought in order to have a place to live while we farmed my mother's land, the money he had brought with him was used up. We could not afford to buy cattle to replace those he had sold in Canada. It was not until nine years after gifting me with his hopeful verse that my husband was able, finally, to place his registered running JN brand on the left hip of cattle once again owned by him, free and clear. Indeed, now, because of a loan from the bank, we own the whole herd to which we have fed hay this winter.

All these years, John's verse has lain on the dresser, a token of his hope, silently declaring the future. As Norman Vincent Peale has said, " ... an image vividly conceived and stubbornly held has a reality of its own."

* * *

After we feed the heifers alfalfa from the rack, John parks it beside the corral next to the steel barn and unhooks Pete and Skeet, leading them to the flat barn for unharnessing. There are some chores yet to do in the yard, and so I begin: I fork alfalfa off the rack and carry it behind the steel barn, where we have a catch-all pen. The milk goats—Nancy and Opal, who are not now giving milk—live in this small lot with an old, arthritic dairy cow, Susie. Pacer lives in this pen, too. He is our young herdsire prospect, a son of Korncrest Pacesetter, the Milking Shorthorn bull to whom I artificially inseminated so many of my mother's dairy cows 30 years ago.

When Pacer was born last spring, I could hardly believe my eyes. His white-red roan color makes him nearly a carbon copy of his sire. Of all the Korncrest Pacesetter calves born to my mother's cows, I cannot recall one being colored so closely to the old bull. Later this summer, Pacer will breed the heifers born to our Mustard Seed Heifers.

Beside Pacer's pen stand two new horses waiting for their alfalfa. They are Tom and Mike, the newest workers on the farm, meant to relieve Pete and Skeet of some of their workload. But Tom and Mike are just big youngsters, coming three years old. They're naive, innocent, blundering. But they will gain their wisdom. Mike, straight black, and Tom, whose blackish coat is sprinkled with grey, are both long-faced and friendly, not easily disturbed. We chose them for our second team because they seem to have the sort of calm temperments that will make them a good team for me to drive, letting me work alongside John and his team in the field as we find more and more ways to tend this land and our cattle using horses as the primary source of power.

When I finish my chores behind the steel barn, I head for the house in time to watch John lead Pete and Skeet across the yard to their night pasture, where piles of alfalfa await them for supper. All three are long-striding. John sets a strong walking pace; to keep up, the horses take big strides, too, their backs swinging, heads low and relaxed. Pete and Skeet look bare and free without their harnesses, though they show no signs of resenting its presence, which envelops them in our purposes. They nicker at John when they see him in the mornings, even when they have plenty of hay. And the more work they do, the easier they are to catch in their roomy paddock where they roam free—and the more personality they express. When John bends down in front of them to pick up the tongue of the wagon, for instance, to hook it to the neckyoke, which is hooked to their collars at the bases of their necks, they both turn their heads inwards and down slightly, in an affectionate acknowledgement of John's presence.

Now, as the unharnessed team walks by me, I see Skeet's patches of bare skin where the harness rubs him ever so slightly. The skin is not raw, just bare, and maybe toughened a bit. John fiddles with Skeet's harness often, trying to adjust it so that it will stop rubbing against his hair, causing a bare patch. But unlike Pete, who has no hair marks from the harness and whose muscles are rounded, Skeet's muscles are bunchy, bulging in awkward places that do not fit the conformity of the harness, no matter which way John adjusts it.

Still, Skeet is not alone. My body is marked, too, from this work on this place. My hands have tough, brown calluses, as do John's. My right forearm is slightly swollen, and my elbow bends stiffly from the pitching. My skin is rough.

I've spent a lot of energy in times past trying to cover life's marks. But hiding external imperfections no longer seems important. I do not mind that my body shows that my life is not physically easy; I do not mind that my possessions reveal that my life is not always comfortable or convenient. It is an inner smoothness that I am after, a sure sense that I am doing the work for which God has marked me . . . and that I am in my proper place.

I have worked on this farm during its high days of a noontide time of financial prosperity, when my body was lithe and my spirit as high as that of the Arabian stallion with whom I raced, windblown, across the fields.

But a time of taming came, and I worked on this farm during its days of silence and slow motion, when its rivers of prosperity dried to a trickle, when its life hung in the balance, tipping more toward death than life. It was a time when I walked on foot.

Now the balance has tipped back again toward life, still precarious, yet nevertheless stirring beneath the surface in new ways, offering the hope of a new kind of life for a new time . . . and a renewed kind of place. My turbulent spirit has grown some peace because, like the wild prairie rose, I am learning to live on arid, unpredictable ground under the arching freedom of God's wide-open skies. The winters here have shown me that—like the biblical prophet Habakkuk—I can trust my faith to God:

"Though the fig tree do not blossom, nor fruit be on the vines, the produce of the olive fail and the fields yield no food, the flock be cut off from the fold and there be no herd in the stalls, yet I will rejoice in the Lord, I will joy in the God of my salvation. God, the Lord, is my strength; he makes my feet like hinds' feet, he makes me tread upon my high places."

RESOURCES FOR READERS

The following publications and organizations are just a few of those offering information relating to alternative living and agriculture.

PUBLICATIONS

ACRES U.S.A.—
A Voice for Eco-Agriculture
P.O. Box 91299
Austin, Texas 78709
(800) 355-5313
www.acresusa.com

Center for Rural Affairs Newsletter
Published by the Center for Rural Affairs
(See address under ORGANIZATIONS)

Holistic Management In Practice
"Providing the link between a healthy environment and a sound economy"
Published by The Allan Savory Center for Holistic Management
(See address under ORGANIZATIONS)

Small Farmer's Journal
"featuring practical Horsefarming"
P.O. Box 1627
Sisters, Oregon 97759
agrarian@smallfarmersjournal.com

Small Farm Today
3903 W. Ridge Trail Rd.

Clark, Missouri 65243
(800) 633-2535
www.smallfarmtoday.com

The Natural Farmer
(Published by the Northeast Organic Farming Association)
c/o Jack Kittredge
411 Sheldon Road
Barre, Massachusetts 01005
tnf@nofaic.org

The Stockman Grass Farmer
P.O. Box 2300
Ridgeland, Mississippi 39158-2300
(800) 748-9808
www.stockmangrassfarmer.com

Wise Traditions in Food, Farming, and the Healing Arts
Published by the Weston A. Price Foundation
(See address under ORGANIZATIONS)

ORGANIZATIONS

Alternative Energy Resources Organization (AERO)
(AERO is a grass-roots group dedicated to sustainable resource use and community vitality.)
432 North Last Chance Gulch
Helena, Montana 59601
(406) 443-7272

Center for Rural Affairs
P.O. Box 406
Walthill, Nebraska 68067-0406
(402) 846-5428
info@cfra.org
www.cfra.org

Land Stewardship Project
(Fosters an ethic of stewardship for farmland, promotes sustainable
agriculture and sustainable communities.)
2200 4th Street
White Bear Lake, Minnesota 55110
(651) 653-0618
www.landstewardshipproject.org

Leopold Center for Sustainable Agriculture
(The Leopold Center explores and cultivates alternatives that secure
healthier people and landscapes in Iowa and the nation.)
209 Curtiss Hall
Iowa State University
Ames, Iowa 50011-1050
(515) 294-3711
leocenter@iastate.edu
www.leopold.iastate.edu

Northern Plains Sustainable Agriculture Society
(NPSAS is a grass-roots educational organization committed to
developing a sustainable society through the promotion of ecologically
and socially sound food-production and -distribution systems in the
Northern Plains.)
9824 79th St. SE
Fullerton, North Dakota 58441-9725

(701) 883-4304
tpnpsas@drtel.net
www.npsas.org

Organic Consumers Association
(OCA provides current information on organic food, food labeling, and
food safety.)
6101 Cliff Estate Rd.
Little Marais, Minnesota 55614
(218) 226-4164
www.organicconsumers.org

The Allan Savory Center for Holistic Management
1010 Tijeras NW
Albuquerque, New Mexico 87102
(505) 842-5252
www.holisticmanagement.org

The Land Institute
(Conducts research in natural-systems agriculture, featuring perennial
grain polycultures using nature as its measure)
2440 E. Water Well Road
Salina, Kansas 67401
(785) 823-5376
www.landinstitute.org

Tillers International
(Dedicated to preserving, studying, and exchanging low-capital
technologies to increase the sustainability and productivity of rural
communities)
10515 East OP Ave.

Scotts, Michigan 49088
(269) 626-0223
tillersox@aol.com
www.wmich.edu/tillers/

Weston A. Price Foundation for Wise Traditions in Food, Farming, and
the Healing Arts
PMB 106-380
4200 Wisconsin Avenue, NW
Washington, D.C. 20016
(202) 333-HEAL
WestonAPrice@msn.com
www.westonaprice.org

WEB SITES

www.ssu.missouri.edu/Faculty/JIkerd
Agricultural economist John Ikerd writes and speaks about issues
relating to sustainable agriculture, with an emphasis on the economics of
sustainability.

www.victoryseeds.com/info_links.html
This site provides links to a number of sustainable and organic
agriculture organizations.

RESOURCES FOR READERS

CONTACT INFORMATION FOR KEY RESOURCES

COVER DESIGNER OF *A Prayer for the Prairie*
Todd Spichke
Riverbrand Design
6145 Dallas Lane North
Plymouth, Minnesota 55446
Ph: (612) 819-5219
Fax: (763) 201-4599
riverbrand@comcast.net

PRINTER of *A Prayer for the Prairie*
Image Printing
1803 E. Broadway Ave.
P.O. Box 696
Bismarck, North Dakota 58502
(800) 307-4001
www.imageprinting.com

TO ORDER

"Feeding the Village First," contact:
The Northern Plains Sustainable Agriculture Society
9824 79th St. SE
Fullerton, North Dakota 58441-9725
(701) 883-4304
tpnpsas@drtel.net
www.npsas.org
No charge

Big Thoughts From a Small Farmer and
Crazy Musings from the North Outback, contact:
Terry Jacobson
9173 95th St. NE
Wales, North Dakota 58281

Nourishing Traditions: The Cookbook that Challenges Politically Correct Nutrition and the Diet Dictocrats, contact:
New Trends Publishing
401 Kings Highway
Winona Lake, Indiana 46590
(877) 707-1776
newtrends@kconline.com
www.newtrendspublishing.com

Catalog of books on organic and sustainable farming and eco-living, contact:
ACRES U.S.A.
P.O. Box 91299
Austin, Texas 78709
(800) 355-5313
www.acresusa.com

SOURCES

Barker, Joel Arthur. *Paradigms: The Business of Discovering the Future.* New York: HarperCollins Publishers, 1992.

Berry, Wendell. *Home Economics.* San Francisco: North Point Press, 1987.

Berry, Wendell. *The Unsettling of America: Culture & Agriculture.* San Francisco: Sierra Club Books, 1977.

Balch, James F., and Phyllis A. Balch. *Prescription for Nutritional Healing.* Garden City, N.Y.: Avery Publishing Group, 1997.

Couplan, Francois. *The Encyclopedia of Edible Plants of North America: Nature's Green Feast.* New Canaan, Conn.: Keats Publishing, 1998.

Duke, James A. *The Green Pharmacy.* Emmaus, Pa.: Rodale Press, 1997.

Kirschenmann, Fred. "Feeding the Village First." Fullerton, N.D.: Northern Plains Sustainable Agriculture Society, 1999.

Savory, Allan. *Holistic Management: A New Framework for Decision Making.* Washington, D.C.: Island Press, 1999.

Sine, Tom. *Wild Hope.* Dallas, Texas: Word Publishing, 1991.

INDEX

ABOUT THE AUTHOR

Raylene Frankhauser Nickel, 50, grew up on a small family farm near Kief, North Dakota. After earning a bachelor's degree with majors in English and psychology, she moved to Manitoba and worked on a purebred cattle ranch for five years. She became a free-lance agricultural journalist in 1984, writing articles for regional and national agricultural magazines in both Canada and the United States. Her writing has won national awards in the realms of agriculture and rural electric cooperatives. In 1990 she moved with her husband, John Nickel, back to North Dakota to the family farm where she worked in her youth.

TO ORDER

A PRAYER FOR THE PRAIRIE

Mail return address and check or money order for
$18.75 U.S. per copy or $26 Canadian
(includes S&H) to:

Five Penny Press
3117 5th Ave. NE
Kief, ND 58723-9500
Phone/fax: (701) 626-7183

* Single orders from North Dakota, enclose $19.69 per copy (includes tax).

* Canadian orders subject to provincial and federal tax.

* For orders of three or more copies to the same address, no S&H charges. Send return address and check or money order for $16.50 U.S. per book; multiple orders from North Dakota, add 5 percent sales tax.

* Special discounts available to volume purchasers such as book clubs, study groups, or other organizations. Contact the publisher for information.